HEAVEN IS VISIBL⬛⬛⬛⬛⬛⬛⬛⬛⬛⬛⬛⬛⬛)

IT HAS GOLDEN CLOUDS
(Job 37:18–22, LXX)

IT IS THE LORD'S THRONE   *(Isaiah 66:1)*

THE LORD'S THRONE IS IN NEW JERUSALEM
(Rev. 18:22:3, 4)

HEAVEN IS CALLED PARADISE
(II Corinthians 12:2–4)

HEAVEN IS A SPHERE   *(Revelation 21:16)*

IT IS A PLANET IN OUR SOLAR SYSTEM
(Psalms 89:36, 37)

HEAVEN IS BETWEEN TWO OTHER PLANETS
(Psalms 99:1)

IT IS A NAKED-EYE PLANET
(Psalms 89:36, 37)

IT HAS A ROCKY CORE   *(Job 38:37, 38, LXX)*

Two of these clues reveal exactly where Heaven
is located.
Do you know which two clues actually solve the
mystery?

HEAVEN FOUND
by M. J. AGEE
REVEALS THE ANSWER . . .

Other Avon Books by
M.J. Agee

THE END OF THE AGE

HEAVEN FOUND

M.J. AGEE

AVON BOOKS NEW YORK

AVON BOOKS
A division of
The Hearst Corporation
1350 Avenue of the Americas
New York, New York 10019

Copyright © 1995 by Marilyn J. Agee
Published by arrangement with Archer Press
Visit our website at **http://AvonBooks.com**
Library of Congress Catalog Card Number: 94-47341
ISBN: 0-380-72699-8

The Archer Press edition contains the following Library of Congress
Cataloging in Publication Data:

Agee, M.J. (Marilyn Jean), 1928–
    Heaven Found : a butter and honey star / by M.J. Agee.
Includes bibliographical references and index.
1. Heaven—Biblical teaching. 2. Eschatology—Biblical teaching.
I. Title
BS680.H42A34 1994   94-47341
236'.24—dc20   CIP

First Avon Books Printing: April 1997

AVON TRADEMARK REG. U.S. PAT. OFF. AND IN OTHER COUNTRIES, MARCA
REGISTRADA, HECHO EN U.S.A.

Printed in the U.S.A.

RA   10   9   8   7   6   5   4   3   2   1

✣

Dedicated to my loving husband, Ed, which means "witness," and to my children, Carol and David, who have all witnessed many miracles that have taken place in our lives since I asked God to show me all that he wanted man to understand about the Bible.

Thou ye have lien among the pots, yet shall ye be as the wings of a dove covered with silver, and her feathers with yellow gold.

Psalm 68:13

He that dwelleth in the secret place of the most High shall abide under the shadow of the Almighty. . . . He shall cover thee with his feathers, and under his wings shalt thou trust.

Psalm 91:1,4

✣ Contents

INTRODUCTION   1

1. HEAVEN: REAL AND VISIBLE   4

2. CHARIOT OF THE CHERUBIM   23

3. THE VENGEANCE OF HIS TEMPLE   68

4. THE SECRET OF HIS TABERNACLE   92

5. THE TABERNACLE PATTERN   139

6. THE MORNING STAR: CHRIST'S THRONE   162

NOTES   195

SELECTED BIBLIOGRAPHY   206

INDEX   210

✠ Introduction

THIS BOOK HAD A MIND OF ITS OWN. AFTER I FIN-
ished *Exit: 2007, The Secret of Secrets revealed* (also
published by Avon Books as *The End of the Age*), I
started writing another book, *The Master Key, Revelation's Secrets Revealed,* explaining the exciting end-of-
the-age drama played out for us in the last book of
the Bible.

When explaining the script in Revelation 4, this
book, *Heaven Found,* outgrew its niche in chapter four
and became a 4-page—6-page—20-page, then a 30-
page report, and finally a full-fledged book in its own
right. Work on *The Master Key* unexpectedly had to be
suspended until this was completed.

Exit: 2007 took over 30 years of intensive Bible study
and 23 years of writing. Because I don't have another 23
years before the Rapture, I knew I had to write the next
book faster, but this one surprised me and sprouted in a
few short months. It is a story that wanted to be told.

1

When I found out God's timing of end-time events, I still had no idea I would ever know in this lifetime where heaven is located. Yet, every time I ran across one of the clues, I kept wondering if it could possibly be where it actually is. It's as if I knew it all along but just wasn't sure until lately.

When I finally got down to business and read several different versions of the Bible specifically searching for clues to where heaven was located, I was able to work it out.

It is so easy, I wonder why no one has figured it out before this. The Lord must have blinded us to it until we entered the time of the end when knowledge is to be increased.

Several clues give it away. It is "as the sun," "as the moon," and "like the earth." It is in the third heaven. There is "brightness round about" it. Mount Sinai and the sapphire symbolize it, but it is actually a rock covered with golden clouds and visible from Earth with the naked-eye. You may have already seen heaven and just not recognized it.

Job 37:18–22 in the Septuagint mentions "the ancient heavens," and says that

> the light is not visible to all; it shines afar off in the heavens, as that which is from him in the clouds. From the north come the clouds shining like gold: in these great are the glory and honour of the Almighty.

The various clues given in Scripture narrow the choices down to one, the pearl of great price, seen slowly and majestically floating along the ecliptic in our night sky. The name of the star of our God even appears in the Bible but was not translated into English.

Heaven will be a morning star when the Rapture takes place. You should be able to pick it out easily on the preceding nights before dawn. It is brighter than the stars in the background constellation Aries, the Ram (suggesting the Lamb of God), which it will just be entering, and Venus, the brightest morning star, will be moving toward conjunction with it.

No wonder Jesus sent this message to the overcomers of the Church Age:

> I will give him the morning star. He that hath an ear, let him hear what the Spirit saith unto the churches (Revelation 2:28,29).

His throne is there. That is why Jesus said that he was the bright and morning star as he signed off in the last chapter of the Bible.

Biblical quotations are from the King James Version unless otherwise noted. For clarity, the first letter in a quotation is not capitalized unless capitalized in the original. Italics in the scriptures are usually omitted so they will not be confused with the bold emphasis I have added throughout.

As you read, "Prove all things; hold fast that which is good." Be sure to compare everything with the scriptures. I may make mistakes, but God never does.

Be sure you have your free ticket to go to heaven, I am convinced that the Rapture of the church will be on a Sunday Pentecost before the turn of the century.

M.J. Agee

1 ✛ Heaven:
Real and Visible

W<small>HEN GAZING UP AT OUR BEAUTIFUL AZURE</small>-blue sky with those majestic white cloud pillows slowly sailing by, did you ever wonder where heaven is?

Were you ever curious enough to try to figure out where Christ went when he ascended? He has ingeniously laid out a celestial road map in the Bible showing us the way not only to eventually go to heaven, but to figure out where it is.

Revelation 21:16 tells us that the heavenly city "lieth foursquare," and that the length, breadth, and height of it are equal. Don't rush out in daylight expecting to see a cube or pyramid tumbling around out there in space, but heaven can be seen with the naked eye.

It is the real "place" Jesus has been preparing for us[1] in an identifiable location. Since the time of the Rapture, when believers are to be taken to heaven, is now near "at hand,"[2] he has made it possible to figure out not only when we are going to take off from this planet, but where we will land.

If you have ever taken the time to really look at the various star patterns in the sky, you may have already caught a glimpse of it on a clear night. When shining steadily in a black-velvet sky, heaven can be seen clearly. Yet, it hovers near the outer limits of what one can see without binoculars or telescope. Viewed through a telescope, it is an object novices and seasoned astronomers alike never cease to marvel at.

Have you ever searched the Bible to see if you can find any clues that would help locate heaven? If you don't try, you won't find them because they are scattered. Miners don't find many opals without digging either. If you do try, you will be amazed at what you can find and will wonder why the location of heaven has gone unrecognized so long. God must have put blinders on us so we would not discover too soon certain secrets he hid in Scripture. He meant for us to find them in the time of the end when knowledge was to be increased.[3]

In Mark 13:23, Jesus said, "I have foretold you **all things.**" All the clues we need are hidden among the pages of Scripture. To gain understanding, we have to look for them. Join me in this search. I am sure there are more hidden clues that are awaiting their proper time to be discovered.

The task is not formidable. The Bible is just one small book. How hard can it be? The only other tool you need is a good concordance so you can locate all the verses that contain a certain word. To start searching for clues that might tell you where heaven is located, begin with things like heaven, paradise, New Jerusalem, throne. You can sort out which passages you want to look up by reading the single line quoted in the reference. The important ones I might want to find quickly later on, I underline with a colored pencil.

I have Cruden's, Young's, and Strong's but find that I use Strong's Concordance the most. In it, you can look up the meanings of original words, which is sometimes necessary to understand all that a passage is trying to tell us. I also use Thayer's Greek-English Lexicon and the Gesenius' Hebrew-Chaldee Lexicon of the Old Testament that is numerically coded to Strong's Exhaustive Concordance for looking up the various meanings of words. However, most of the time, Strong's is enough. It is my most valuable reference book.

When the translators did not understand the full import of what was being said, the word chosen may not be quite as clear as another equally-correct choice would be. This is particularly true when a word has multiple meanings.

The search is like solving a mystery. You have to think like a detective. Look for clues and put two and two together. Say to yourself, since this is so, then that must be so.

A Butter and Honey Star

On a clear dark night, to the unassisted eye, heaven looks like a star that glows with pearl-white light. It moves very slowly through the constellations along the ecliptic, the apparent path of the sun among the stars.

This eliminates a lot of heavenly bodies that do not trace the sun's path. Actually, besides the sun and moon, there are only five naked-eye objects that shine brighter than most of the the other stars and yet travel in front of the seemingly stationary background stars.

Heaven is one of them. It is the Lord's throne. Gold is a symbol of deity. As befits our Lord Jesus Christ, heaven is wrapped in thick golden clouds, which may be why the streets are washed with transparent gold.

Seen through a powerful space telescope, the texture reminds me of cotton candy twirled on a paper cone, but the coloring resembles a ball of whipped butter with a brush dipped in flowing honey held lightly against it as it turns. The honey thins over the swollen equatorial zone and runs thick into narrow amber V-shaped belts dividing the equatorial from the temperate zones. A dry edge of the brush brings up the equatorial color in a thin band at the top of the temperate zone before the polar caps fade into amber then cinnamon.

Heaven's position in relation to the Earth changes from time to time, but the astronomers have prepared charts that show you where in the sky to look for it on certain dates. However, before you dash out to the library to check the charts, you'll have to find out what our astronomers call it.

Not Everyone Has Seen Heaven

Although easily visible to the unaided eye, heaven has not been seen by everyone. It is far from the Earth and is not the brightest star in the sky. (That quickly cuts the list to four possibilities.) The light reaches Earth, but is dim enough not to be noticed by everyone. In the Septuagint (LXX), the Greek scriptures used in Jesus' time, Job 36:32; 37:3, and 37:18–22 make this clear:

He has hidden the light in his hands, and given charge concerning it to the interposing cloud . . . His dominion is under the whole heaven, and **his**

light is at the extremities of the earth (so his light reaches Earth).

Wilt thou establish with him foundations for the ancient heavens? . . . But **the light is not visible to all; it shines afar off in the heavens,** as that which is from him in the clouds. From the north come the **clouds shining like gold** (i.e., visible): in these great are the glory and honour of the Almighty.

Heaven has an exceptionally thick cloud cover. This eliminates two more objects from the list. Only two remain. The color of the clouds actually zeroes in on one, but I cannot reveal its name until we can examine Scripture's clues carefully and prove each step as we go. Otherwise, you wouldn't be sure that the conclusion drawn was true.

Glory and honor belong to the throne of the Almighty. Scripture tells it over and over. The "LORD made the heavens. Honour and majesty are before him: strength and beauty are in his sanctuary."[4] "Who is this King of glory? The LORD of hosts, he is the King of glory."[5]

The Throne of the First and the Last

The glorious clouds shining like gold envelop the throne of Jesus Christ. He is the Son of God. He also is the Lord of hosts, the King of glory, and the Almighty.

Isaiah 9:6 says that "his name shall be called Wonderful, Counsellor, The mighty God, The everlasting Father, The Prince of Peace." Stop and think about each of those names. It is an impressive list of his credentials.

Is he "The everlasting Father?"

Of course. If the Scripture says it, it's true. The New Testament agrees. Second Corinthians 5:18 clearly says, "God was in Christ, reconciling the world unto himself."

In the Revelation of Jesus Christ, he tells us with his own mouth who he really is. If we did not quite understand it before, here, in the last book of the Bible, he stands revealed. It is His Revelation. The message in chapter 1:5,8 is from "Jesus Christ . . . the first begotten of the dead . . . that loved us, and washed us from our sins in his own blood." He said,

> **I am Alpha and Omega, the beginning** (Yahweh) **and the ending** (*Y'shua, Iesous,* Jesus, which means Yahweh is saviour), saith the Lord, which is (at the Rapture) and which was (at the First Advent), and which is to come (at the Second Advent), **the Almighty.**

If we missed that, he tells us one last time in the thirteenth verse of the last chapter of the Bible:

> I am Alpha and Omega, the beginning and the end, **the first and the last.**

As the pre-incarnate Christ, he was the first—the Lord of the Old Testament. As the incarnate Christ, he is the last—the Lord of the New Testament. First Corinthians 15:47 says,

> The first man (Adam) is of the earth, earthy: the second man (Christ) **is the Lord from heaven.**

Jesus Christ has two complete natures. He is both man and God. Isaiah 9:6 helps us understand how he came to have these two natures. "For unto us a child is born, unto us a son is given." The child was born of Mary. He inherited his manhood from her. He inherited his Godhood from his Father.

The Heaven

God named the stars. Psalms 147:4 says, "He telleth the number of the stars; he calleth them all by their names."

Our heavenly home, sometimes referred to in the Bible as "the heaven," as apposed to the "heaven of heavens," is a literal place with a name. It is where New Jerusalem and "the throne of God and of the Lamb"[6] are located.

But who is able to build him an house, seeing **the heaven** and heaven of heavens cannot contain him?[7]

Thou, even thou, art LORD alone; thou hast made **heaven,** the heaven of heavens, with all their host, the earth, and all things that are therein.[8]

THUS saith the LORD, **The heaven** is my throne, and the earth is my footstool.[9]

The heaven, even the heavens, are the LORD'S: but the earth hath he given to the children of men.[10]

Have you ever noticed how heaven is mentioned over and over in the same sentence as the Earth. We know Earth is real. Use your powers of deduction. If Earth is real, heaven is real. There actually are many more correlations between heaven and Earth, and we will find some of them as we search the scriptures for clues.

The Third Heaven

Paul gave us a good solid clue to where our heaven is located in Second Corinthians 12:2–4 when he said,

> I knew a man in Christ above fourteen years ago, (whether in the body, I cannot tell; or whether out of the body, I cannot tell: God knoweth;) such an one caught up to the **third heaven.** And I knew such a man . . . How that he was caught up into **paradise.**

Paradise is in "the third heaven." There can be no doubt. What else ties in with paradise? Use your concordance. The "tree of life . . . is in the midst of the paradise of God."[11] Look up the tree of life. You will find that it is in the heavenly city, New Jerusalem.[12] Therefore New Jerusalem, our heavenly home, is paradise and is in the third heaven.

This should have told me where our heaven was located long ago, but the truth was obscured by this note in my Scofield Bible: "First heaven, of clouds; second, of stars; third, God's abode." They haven't even changed it much in the New Scofield Reference Bible. It says, "The 'third heaven' is the abode of God, the first heaven being that of the clouds, and the second heaven that of the stars."

Someone must have imagined that one somewhere along the way. The third is God's abode, but the first heaven has nothing to do with clouds as in our atmosphere, and the second would cover a very unequal amount of space if it included all the stars that burn with atomic fires like our sun. Our atmosphere is next to nothing compared to the size of the universe outside of our solar system.

A Celestial Sphere

Heaven is not only real and in an identifiable location, but it is also inhabited at the present time by people who have previously lived on Earth. We know for certain that Enoch, Noah, Abraham and Sarah are alive[13] and have taken up residence in New Jerusalem, the same heavenly city that we will be taken to when the Rapture takes place.[14] The writer of the letter to the Hebrews explained in chapter eleven that

> (Abraham) looked for a city which hath foundations, whose builder and maker is God.

The city with foundations is New Jerusalem. It is unusual in that it has twelve foundations.[15] As the passage in Hebrews continues, it is speaking of Enoch, Noah, Abraham and Sarah.

> These all died in faith . . . and confessed that they were strangers (*zenoi;* **aliens**) and pilgrims (*parepidemoi;* aliens alongside) on the earth. For they that say such things declare plainly that they seek a country (*patrida;* fatherland). And truly, if they had been mindful of that country from whence they came out (Earth), they might have had opportunity to have returned. But now they desire **a better country,** that is, an **heavenly:** wherefore God is not ashamed to be called their God: for he hath prepared for them a city.[16]

These are real people in a real place. Jesus said, "I go to prepare a place for you."[17] It is the heavenly New Jerusalem where the throne of God and the Lamb

is located. It is the fatherland that is described for us
in Revelation 21:

> And the city lieth foursquare . . . **The length and
> the breadth and the height of it are equal** . . .
> and the city was pure gold, like unto clear
> glass. . . . The throne (singular) of God and of
> the Lamb (one person, Jesus Christ, who is both
> God and the Lamb) shall be in it; and his (one
> person's) servants shall serve him; And they shall
> see his face (one face); and his name (one name)
> shall be in their foreheads.[18]

What kind of geometrical shape is this city? a cube?
a pyramid? I doubt it. To me, it just does not make
sense. When we train our most powerful telescopes on
other large bodies floating around out there in space,
we do not see a single cube or pyramid shape among
them. What do we see? Here a sphere, there a sphere,
and everywhere a sphere.

Christ is a high priest after the order of Melchisedec,[19] and the Levites were priests. Levitical cities
were round with an inner and an outer suburb surrounding them.[20] These cities of refuge could easily be
types of heaven. If so, their circles within circles could
be an excellent clue we should not ignore.

I believe that New Jerusalem is a sphere. "The
length and the breadth and the height of it are equal,"
perfect dimensions for a globe floating through space
on a breath of wind.

"Oh, but it's foursquare,"[21] you say. Yes, and when
the astronauts photographed the Earth from space, you
saw its "four corners" and "four wings" didn't you?
Look at these scriptures.

He shall . . . gather those dispersed from Judah, from the **four wings of the earth** (Isaiah 11:12, Green's Interlinear Hebrew/Greek-English Bible).

And he shall . . . gather together the dispersed of Judah from the **four corners** (*kanaph*) **of the earth** (Isaiah 11:12, KJV).

I saw four angels standing on the **four corners** (*gonias*) **of the earth,** holding the four winds of the earth, that the wind should not blow on the earth (Revelation 7:1, KJV).

What these scriptures actually mean finally comes clear when you read Revelation 20:8 in the King James Version:

And shall go out to deceive the nations which are in the **four quarters** (*gonias,* the word translated 'corners' above) **of the earth.**

Both the Hebrew word *kanaph* and the Greek word *gonias* can be translated as "wings," "corners," or "quarters."

The astronomical symbol for Earth is a circle divided into four quarters. This furnishes us a good clue.

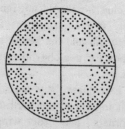

Imagine an orange with the rind scored into quarters. These quarters are its wings. Two cover one side and two the other side. The same is true of the cherubim in Ezekiel 1:23. There, "every one had two, which covered on this side, and every one had two, which covered on that side, their bodies." Later, we'll find a good reason for this correlation.

The symbolism of wings is great for the Earth is actually flying at breakneck speed. It is hurtling through space at 18.51 miles **per second** outdoing some modern rocketry.

A Naked-Eye Object in Our Solar System

Heaven, the Lord's throne, is in our own solar system and is definitely visible as a naked-eye object. Psalms 89:36,37 speaks of David's seed, which is Christ. It says his throne is "as the sun" and "as the moon," the two brightest and most visible spheres in this solar system:

> His seed shall endure for ever, and his throne **as the sun** before me. It shall be established for ever **as the moon,** and as a faithful witness (and therefore visible) **in heaven.**

His throne is not the sun, but "as" the sun. It is not the moon, but "as" the moon. This is figurative language. Since the Lord said the sun is "**before me,**" his throne must be farther out in the solar system than the sun. This even sounds like it might orbit the sun. If it did, the sun would continually be before him.

A major clue is that heaven is also like the Earth. We feel comfortable with this comparison for we know more about the planet on which we live than we do about any other heavenly body. In Psalms 78:69, we find that the Lord

> built his sanctuary (tabernacle) like high palaces (planets), **like the earth** (a planet).

Therefore, heaven is a planet in our own solar system, and it does orbit the sun.

There are several ways of eliminating the number of choices possible for heaven until we are left with one. The more ways we work it out, the more convincing the result, for the different pathways all lead to the same end.

Out of millions of points of light spattered across the sky, knowing that heaven is a planet in our own solar system cuts our choices considerably. There are a total of nine planets, but the Earth is excluded. Therefore, instead of heaven being anywhere out there among the stars that cannot be numbered, it is one of just eight possibilities.

POSSIBILITIES

Mercury Venus Mars Jupiter Saturn Uranus Neptune Pluto

AND HEAVEN IS AMONG THEM

Heaven is a Rock

Our astronomers have wondered whether or not this particular planet has a rocky core. Since it is always covered with thick clouds, we cannot see its surface. In the Septuagint, Job 38:37,38 says,

(Who) is he that numbers the clouds in wisdom, and has bowed the heaven . . . to the earth? For it (heaven) is spread out **as dusty earth,** and **I have cemented it as one hewn stone to another.**

Since stones are cemented together, heaven has a rocky surface. It sounds like the Lord formed it by coalescence. This should make the astronomers happy, because it seems to confirm their theory that the planets were formed of planetesimals that later coalesced to form the planets. This is probably also why they are all spheres. Each piece is as close to the center of gravity as it can get.

Four Mysteries

There are four very mysterious things in the Bible that have long defied complete explanation:

(1) "the chariot of the cherubims"
(2) "the vengeance of his temple"
(3) "the noise of his tabernacle"
(4) "the secret of his tabernacle"

When we unravel these mysteries, we can understand more clearly the clues that show where heaven is. All four tie-in with either the tabernacle Moses built at Mt. Sinai in the wilderness after the Israelites came out of Egypt or with the temple King David's son, Solomon, built on the threshingfloor of Ornan the Jebusite on Mount Moriah at Jerusalem.

The tabernacle Moses pitched symbolized things in the heavens, including the cherubim,[22] the flaming sword,[23] and the throne of God and of the Lamb.[24] Jesus Christ is the high priest, who is set on the right hand of the throne of the Majesty in the heavens; A minister of the sanctuary, and of **the true tabernacle,** which the Lord pitched, and not man. . . . Who serve unto the **example** (*hupodeigmati;* representation, pattern, example) and **shadow of heavenly things.**[25]

According to Hebrews 9:23,24, the tabernacle contained "patterns of things in the heavens . . . which are the figures of the true." The Greek word *hupodeigmata,* translated "patterns," also means representations. The tabernacle contained representations of things in the heavens. They are the *antitupa,* antitypes or counterparts, of the real things.

Have you wondered why the ten curtains that covered the tabernacle were embroidered with cherubim? It is because they represented ten cherubim that fly in our heavens.

(God) sitteth upon the circle (*chuwg;* circuit, i.e., orbit) of the earth . . . stretcheth out the heavens **as a curtain,** and spreadeth them out as a tent **to dwell in.**[26]

There is much to be learned from everything about the tabernacle. It represents "things in the heavens" and identifies the "star" of our God, his dwelling place.

Scripture tells us that God "**sitteth between the cherubims,**"[27] and that "the LORD of hosts . . . is **enthroned on the cherubim.**"[28] Since the Lord's throne is in New Jerusalem[29] and he is enthroned on the cherubim, New Jerusalem is on a cherubim located between two others.

This shows us right away that a cherubim must be a planet. Because he sits between cherubim, it also eliminates the two outer planets, Mercury and Pluto, from our lineup of possibilities. There are now only six choices left in this list.

See how easy it is? We have gotten far in a very short time. All it takes is a little sleuthing.

The Tabernacle Tells a Story

The Lord's original instruction manual for building the tabernacle was detailed, and Moses was warned to make all things according to the pattern shown him on the mount. It was important that he follow the exact specifications because the tabernacle told a story. However, to my knowledge, the last page of that scroll has never before been unrolled.

Many things about the tabernacle, its furnishings, and the feasts celebrated there point to Christ. Some of the more obvious associations are easy to make. Gold represents his deity, and his glory shines throughout. He is the bread of life, the light of the world, our passover, the firstfruit, and the door by which we enter heaven. However, more is depicted by the tabernacle than we ever thought possible—much more.

In the past, after reading some books about the tabernacle, I laid them down thinking that just about every single part of it related to Christ, right down to the sockets. In a way that is true. It relates to his throne, his person, his holiness, his power, his creation, his decisions, his actions, his laws, his sacrifice, etc. However, not one of those books ever hinted that the tabernacle might have some secret to tell us about where heaven is located. Yet Psalms 27:5 says,

In the time of (Jacob's) trouble he shall hide me in his pavilion (*cok,* tabernacle): in **the secret of his tabernacle** (*ohel,* tent, 'as *clearly* **conspicuous from a distance**'[30]) shall he hide me; he shall set me up upon **a rock.**

First Corinthians 10:4 says that in the wilderness, the Israelites "drank of that spiritual Rock that followed them: and that Rock was Christ," but if a saint is to be hidden in **his pavilion** up upon a rock, he won't put his feet on the Lord.

This rock is not symbolic, but literal. Its location is the secret hidden in his tabernacle. If it is clearly conspicuous from Earth, it is striking enough to attract attention and obvious to the eye if we know where and when to look for it.

Since the saved are to be set up upon a rock, and they are to be taken to New Jerusalem where His throne is, which is on a cherubim, a cherubim is a rock.

In Ezekiel's visions, the cherubim are called living creatures, but that is because the translators did not know what they represented. The passage is figurative. They are literally *chajoth,* lively things. (More about the cherubim later.)

Why God Teaches With Symbols

Have you wondered why God shrouded some information in so much mystery? why he used symbols, veiled figures, and layers of meaning? Putting together the prophetic picture is like working a jigsaw puzzle. The pieces are mixed up and scattered all over the table. We have to look at each one of them and figure out where it fits in the big picture.

I thank the Lord for the book of Revelation. It is an

outline that helps us get the sequence of events right. Those obscure Old Testament prophecies fit right into it.

Remember. Jesus said, "But take ye heed: behold, I have foretold you all things."[31] All the clues we need to figure everything out had to be planted in Scripture, but some things were certainly not meant to be understood immediately.

Isaiah 28:13 shows why. The word of the Lord is here a little and there a little so the unbeliever will not understand and will therefore come into judgment. Isaiah said,

> Whom shall he teach knowledge? and whom shall he make to understand doctrine? them that are weaned from the milk, and drawn from the breasts. . . . the word of the LORD was unto them precept upon precept . . . line upon line . . . here a little, and there a little; that they might go, and fall backward, and be broken, and snared, and taken.[32]

The way of salvation is plain; believe in the Lord Jesus Christ and thou shalt be saved. Paul made it clear. He said,

> If thou shalt confess with thy mouth the Lord Jesus, and shalt believe in thine heart that God hath raised him from the dead, thou shalt be saved.[33]

Interpreting prophecy is harder. Faith in Christ must come first. When we first accept Christ as our Saviour, our sins are forgiven and we are filled with His Holy Spirit. Only then we can begin to understand the deeper things hidden in the Scriptures for they are spiritually discerned.

It takes the indwelling Holy Spirit to be able to fully comprehend what the tabernacle depicts. When you discover the secret it's been hiding all these years, you may be shocked.

Clues

Heaven is visible (Job 37:18–22, LXX).
It has golden clouds (Job 37:18–22, LXX).
It is the Lord's throne (Isaiah 66:1).
The Lord's throne is in New Jerusalem (Rev. 18; 22:3,4).
Heaven is called Paradise (II Corinthians 12:2–4).
Paradise is in the third heaven (II Corinthians 12:2–4).
Heaven is a sphere (Revelation 21:16).
It is a planet in our solar system (Psalms 89:36,37).
Heaven is between two other planets (Psa. 99:1).
It is a naked-eye planet (Psalms 89:36,37).
It has a rocky core (Job 38:37,38, LXX).

Two of these clues reveal exactly where heaven is located if we know enough facts about our own solar system. Do you know which two clues actually solve the mystery?[34]

2 ✦ Chariot of the Cherubim

THE CHARIOT OF THE CHERUBIM, IS IT REAL OR symbolic? and what about cherubim themselves? How can they represent planets? That goes against everything we have been taught about them. Surely cherubim and seraphim are beings of an angelic order.

If the true meaning of the cherubim was a hard knot to untie, the chariot of the cherubim was much harder. The words, "chariot of the cherubims" only appear once in Scripture.

When king David gathered the materials together for his son Solomon to use in building the temple in Jerusalem, he gave

gold for the **pattern of the chariot of the cherubims,** that spread out their wings, and covered the ark of the covenant of the LORD. All this, said David, the LORD made me understand in

writing by his hand upon me, even all the works
of this pattern (I Chronicles 28:18).

David understood all the works of this figure but did
not spell it out for us. We have to solve that mystery too.

It is strange that this chariot was not mentioned when
the instructions were given to construct the Ark, mercy
seat and cherubim in the tabernacle. Here, it seems that
David was given understanding beyond what Moses
possessed. The Psalms he wrote back this up. The Lord
has revealed his truths to mankind in steps. In Psalm
119:99–105, David said

**I have more understanding than all my teach-
ers:** for thy testimonies are my meditation. **I understand more than the ancients**. . . . How
sweet are thy words unto my taste! yea, sweeter
than honey to my mouth! Through thy precepts I
get understanding . . . Thy word is a lamp unto
my feet, and a light unto my path.

David was a man after the Lord's own heart because he
confessed his sin and applied himself to a study of the
Lord's word. We can do the same thing. He has shown
us the way. He earned the right to rule again. He will be
resurrected and placed on his own throne under Christ.

I the LORD will be their God, and my servant
David a prince among them; I the LORD have
spoken it.[1]

But they shall serve the LORD their God, and
David their king, whom I will raise up unto
them.[2]

And . . . my servant David shall be their prince for ever.[3]

Solving the Puzzle

Let's tackle the cherubim first. If we do not understand that they actually represent the planets, we have very little chance of figuring out what the chariot of the cherubim represents. The usual interpretation is that cherubim are one group in the hierarchy of angelic beings. I accepted that for many years, but I do not think it is correct. I'll show you why.

Visualizing Ezekiel's Cherubim

Ezekiel had two visions of cherubim. He described them in chapters one and ten. The way the King James Version is translated, I at first assumed that they were living creatures with bodies like a man, except that they have four different faces, four wings that are joined one to another, and feet like a calf's foot.

That figure is not too hard to visualize until you find out that the four faces were of a man, a lion, an ox and an eagle. If you start with the shape of an eagle, how could one side of it look like a lion? Without the shape of a lion's head, how would you recognize the fact that it was a lion? The same goes for the ox, and the man. And what about the difference in size between the lion face and the eagle face? It seems to me that you would almost have to have four heads joined into one or you would have trouble recognizing the faces, but nothing is said in either the first or tenth chapters of Ezekiel about them having four heads.

Then to add to my confusion, Ezekiel 1:13 says that they look like burning coals of fire or lamps. How can living creatures with bodies like a man look like burning coals? I thought, "What do we have here? constellations? The stars are burning atomic furnaces. No, these are living creatures."

Before I could figure that out, I found that they have wheels that work together in such a way that they seem to be a wheel in the middle of a wheel. That is puzzling. Is each in turn reduced in size so that it fits inside the wheel of another?

This would place the cherubim inside the wheel structure for Ezekiel 10:9 says that one wheel is by one cherub, and another wheel is by another cherub.

Next, the living creatures seemed to be spirits for Ezekiel 1:20 says, "Whithersoever the spirit was to go, they went, thither was their spirit to go. However, in the next verse, I found that "the spirit of the living creature was in the wheels." Something was wrong with my visualization. How could a spirit with the likeness of a man be in each of the wheels within wheels? And these wheels spin rapidly for verse 14 says that the "living creatures ran and returned as the appearance of a flash of lightning." That is fast.

"Hold it," I thought, "put on the brakes. It's time to go back and read this more carefully. I must have misunderstood something along the way." Yes! I misunderstood so badly that I missed the whole significance of the visions.

I turned to books from BIOLA's[4] library. Someone must know what this means. However, they didn't seem to make a whole lot of sense to me when they got to the cherubim. In all this time since the Old Testament days when Ezekiel wrote this, hadn't anyone unravelled the meaning?

Cherubim: Accepted Interpretation

Concerning a cherub or the cherubim, under the heading "The Meaning," Unger's Bible Dictionary says, "The cherubim seem to be actual beings of the angelic order." That is the accepted interpretation. Many think of the angelic order as including angels, archangels, cherubim and seraphim.

However, under the heading "Form," Unger's Bible Dictionary says,

> Undoubtedly we are to think of the cherub as at Byblos; that is, as a winged lion with human face. In any case, they are celestial creatures belonging to the spiritual realm and not at all to be confounded with any natural identification.

What about Ezekiel's statement that "they had the likeness of a man?"[5] What about the four faces? And not to be confounded with any natural identification— that kind of thinking tends to turn down the power to our brains, so we won't even try to find out if there is a secret embodied in the cherubim and the chariot of the cherubim.

In his effort to scramble our understanding, Satan strews all kinds of confusing counterfeits along the path to truth. We can't look to those things for answers. Scripture must be allowed to speak for itself and interpret itself.

Hidden Secrets Are to be Revealed

We must be open minded, curious, alert, and not let anything close the door to inquiry, no matter how well intended. God meant for us to use the intelligence he gave us. He created us with the brains to figure out what he is telling us, no matter how veiled, as long as we are believers indwelt by his Holy Spirit. He didn't give us any scriptures just to fill up space. Everything we are told in the Bible is for a reason.

When we keep asking ourselves why we need to know something, we will uncover new truths. The Bible has many hidden things to disclose to us, but we have to search for clues and solve puzzles along the way. If we pray and keep on searching, it will yield secret after secret. No matter how high the step we are on, there always seems to be one more.   .

In Mark 4:22–25, Jesus said that unto those who have, more will be given,

> **For there is nothing hid, which shall not be manifested; neither was any thing kept secret, but that it should come abroad.** If any man have ears to hear, let him hear. And he said unto them, Take heed what ye hear: with what measure ye mete, it shall be measured to you: and unto you that hear shall more be given. For he that hath, to him shall be given: and he that hath not, from him shall be taken even that which he hath.

The Search

I have found the scripture, "For he that hath, to him shall be given," to be very true. When I started Bible study in earnest, I had no idea where it would lead. That beginning and where I am today are light years apart. Every time I think I know most of it, a new subject to pursue emerges. There seems to be no end to what we can dig out if we keep trying.

Even when I figured out God's Timetable of End-

Time Events, I still had no idea I would ever know in this lifetime where heaven is located. I had run across some of the clues and had even wondered if it could be where they seemed to point, yet I did not have enough evidence gathered together to convince me. It's like I knew it already, but didn't believe it. I just tacked it back there in my brain and wondered about it from time to time. I'd say to myself, "Is it possible?" but I didn't get any farther than that for a long time.

All through 34 years of intensive Bible study I kept thinking to myself that the tabernacle might mean more than people realized. I came back to it over and over again, but was not able to get a clear enough picture to be sure until lately.

The Lord leads us a step at a time. I seldom sit down to write about the treasures I have uncovered but I find that I know more than I thought I knew. It's uncanny. I learn more as I write. My mind makes new connections. Somehow, he opens your eyes as you go and increases your understanding.

The more you know about the Bible as a whole, the more you will see in individual passages. Reading as many translations as possible has helped me tremendously.

You just have to be willing and get started. He will guide you all along the way. He is in you and can influence your thoughts. Like a good teacher, he doesn't do it for you, but helps you figure it out for yourself. And boy, do I get a rush when I understand one new thing. I purse my lips and blow softly, and the hair stands up on my arms.

I'm amazed time and time again at how much he has packed into that one small book. No man could have done it. To me, that proves the scriptures are God-breathed. Fulfilled prophecy proves it too. His prophecies come true 100%.

Among all the other interesting Biblical subjects I was pursuing, I tried to find out what the cherubim were by reading man's books about the Bible. For seven years I tried hard to learn as much about the whole Bible as possible. I read constantly. I checked out a stack of books about 18" high from the library of the Bible Institute of Los Angeles every week.

I learned a lot, but it didn't work where the cherubim were concerned. Either the authors left the part about the cherubim out or went off on a fanciful trip that I knew couldn't be right. Not only did no one seem to know what the cherubim were, but I couldn't even find out for sure what the word itself meant or where it came from.

Strong's Concordance says the Hebrew word *keruwb* is "of uncert. der.; a *cherub* or imaginary figure:— cherub, [plur.] cherubims." Young's Concordance says *kerub* means "One grasped, held fast," but from reading the discussion in Gesenius' Lexicon, this definition even seems shaky. Gesenius confessed, "The etymology of the word is doubtful."

Lord, Show Me

I don't deny that the books I read helped me understand the Bible. They did me a world of good. I gained a good working knowledge of the Bible as a whole, and that background is indispensable.

However, research on certain subjects like the cherubim, the curse, and the flaming sword led to so many dead ends that finally, in exasperation, I opened my Bible, put my hands on it and said, "Lord! You'll have to show me! I want to know everything you want man to know about the Bible, all the deep things, everything!'' From that time on, I read the Bible itself far more than books written about the Bible. Every time I start over, I try to obtain a different translation. It helps.

"Be Still and Know That I Am God"

One night after that, I woke up suddenly and was absolutely terrified, not knowing why. My heart was beating like a little bird trying to get out of my chest.

Right away, I heard a masculine voice say, ''Be still and know that I am God.'' My heart quieted instantly. Awestruck, I didn't move until after daybreak, but nothing else happened. Twenty years rolled by before I understood what took place that night.

I was reading Job 33 in the Septuagint when it finally dawned on me that when God spoke to me, he somehow opened my understanding. It was after that incident that I really started to be able to figure out the hard things that no one else seemed to know. The passage I was reading says,

> For when the Lord speaks once, or a second time,
> sending a dream, or in the meditation of the night;
> (as **when a dreadful alarm happens to fall upon
> men, in slumberings on the bed:) then opens he
> the understanding of men** (Job 33:15,16, LXX).

This parenthetic portion is not mine. It is not editorial comment, but part of the Scripture. The emphasis is mine.

Digging out the deep things hasn't come easy. The Lord didn't just lay it on me. I ran to do my work so I could get back to my Bible study. I have worked hard and done without enough sleep. Many new things have been learned around 3:00 o'clock in the morning. Something new would come clear. Then I would mark my place, know exactly where to start the next day, and finally tumble into bed.

In some passages, like the first part of Ezekiel chapter one, I looked up nearly every word in the original to try to get some heading as to what it was really about.

Between Earth and Heaven

I believe that the cherubim have a natural identification. In the past, we have just failed to recognize what it is.

Cherubim and a flaming sword are first mentioned in Genesis 3:24, when Adam was exiled from the Garden of Eden. This is one of the scriptures I desperately wanted to understand and could not find anyone who could tell me what it really meant. I now know what both the cherubim and the flaming sword represent. They are both real things in the heavens. Genesis 3:24 says that God

> drove out the man; and he placed at the east of the garden of Eden **Cherubims,** and a **flaming sword** which turned every way, to keep the way (*derek,* path) of (to[6]) the tree of life.[7]

Since the word ''Cherubims'' is plural, there have to be at least two placed east of the Garden of Eden. Also, when our creator said that the flaming sword turned every way, he knew exactly what he was talking about. When you find out what it represents, you will immediately recognize the fact that the flaming sword literally does turn in every direction.

Skipping to the Bible's last chapter, we find that the tree of life that disappeared from the earthly Garden of

Eden is now in the heavenly Paradise. There is an earthly Garden of Eden and a heavenly Garden of Eden. Therefore, the cherubim and the flaming sword do not have to be on the Earth.

That knowledge came as a surprise to me, for I had assumed that they were positioned to the east of Eden on the ground, but this scripture does not limit them to the Earth at all. They were merely said to be placed to the east of the Garden of Eden. That could include the sky. Actually, they can appear out there in the great expanse of space anywhere between Earth and the heavenly "throne of God and of the Lamb."

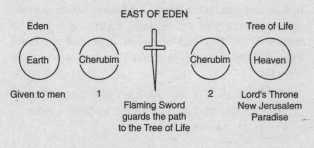

EAST OF EDEN

Eden — Earth — Given to men

Cherubim — 1

Flaming Sword guards the path to the Tree of Life

Cherubim — 2

Tree of Life — Heaven — Lord's Throne New Jerusalem Paradise

I Chronicles 21:16 graphically demonstrates that the Sword of the Lord is between Earth and heaven. It says,

> David lifted up his eyes, and saw the angel of the LORD (this is the pre-incarnate Christ) stand **between the earth and the heaven, having a drawn sword in his hand.**

Real Celestial Objects

Both cherubim and the flaming sword are symbols of real celestial objects, and probably everyone with good vision has seen the brightest cherubim on a clear night. Remember the saying we said as children—Star light, star bright, first star I've seen tonight? That star was very likely the brightest cherubim. When it is floating by in the inky sky, it outshines everything else except our moon.

Five cherubim are visible to the unaided eye. It is possible to see the rest and the flaming sword with modern telescopic equipment.

Standing Guard Duty

Since the tree of life is now in heaven, and nothing that defiles can enter heaven, it makes sense that the flaming sword was set between Earth and heaven to keep the evil that had just been unleashed on Earth from also defiling heaven. Jesus Christ said,

> And there shall in no wise enter into it any thing that defileth, neither whatsoever worketh abomination, or maketh a lie.[8]

The flaming sword is like a military guard. It is stationed where it can guard the path to the tree of life in the heavenly Paradise. No evil man was to be allowed to enter heaven where the throne of God and the Lamb are located.

Drawn From The Sheath

The flaming sword is also called the glittering sword in Scripture. Deuteronomy 32:41,42 gives us an idea how the Lord will use it on the Day of God's Wrath after the present age ends and the Millennium begins on the Feast of Trumpets.

If I whet my glittering sword, and mine hand take hold on judgment; I will render vengeance to mine enemies, and will reward them that hate me. I will make mine arrows drunk with blood, and my sword shall devour flesh; and that with the blood of the slain and of the captives, from the beginning of revenges upon the enemy.

The beginning of revenges refers to the Day of God's Wrath. When the multinational army attacks Israel, God's fury will come up in his face, and all the world will shake as a result. Many think this is Armageddon, but it is only the beginning of revenges. Armageddon will follow Christ's return, which is seven months later.[9] Satan's army will be pitted against Christ's army, and you know who will win.

The glittering sword will literally become a flaming sword as it enters our atmosphere. Ezekiel 21:28–30 explains this and ties it in to Eden. It says,

The sword, the sword is drawn: for the slaughter it is furbished, to consume because of the glittering . . . upon . . . the wicked, whose day is come, when their iniquity shall have an end. Shall I cause it to return into his sheath? I will judge thee in the place where thou wast created, in the land of thy nativity.

The place where man was created was in Eden. That is the land that had a curse put on it, and that is where the flaming sword will strike. Because of Adam's sin, the Lord drove them out and said," . . . cursed is the ground for thy sake."[10]

Location of The Garden of Eden

Eden was near the spot where the Euphrates River flows into the Persian Gulf. Halley's Bible Handbook quotes an interesting ancient Babylonian inscription that shows that the Garden of Eden was near Eridu, twelve miles south of Ur, the city where Abraham grew up.

> Near Eridu was a garden, in which was a mysterious Sacred Tree, a Tree of Life, planted by the gods, whose roots were deep, while its branches reached to heaven, protected by guardian spirits, and no man enters.''[11]

The War Chariot

Understanding one thing often hinges upon figuring out something else. Identifying the flaming sword is easier if we first figure out exactly what the cherubim and ''the chariot of the cherubims'' represent.

Unger's Bible Dictionary says that the chariot of the cherubim probably means ''the cherubim as the chariot upon which God enters or is throned.'' That's a good educated guess, but the picture is hazy. By studying the tabernacle, we can get a clearer view.

It is not clear what the chariot of the cherubim represents when it is mentioned in I Chronicles 28. This is one of those mysteries we have to solve. A pattern of the chariot of the cherubim was in the temple, and therefore also in the earlier tabernacle that Moses built. As we have already seen, David gave Solomon

> gold for the **pattern** (*tabniyth,* figure) **of the chariot** (*merkabah,* war chariot) **of the cherubims,** that spread out their wings, and covered

the ark of the **covenant** of the LORD. All this, said David, the LORD made me understand in writing by his hand upon me, even all the works (*melakah*) of this pattern.[12]

Looking up the original word for chariot gives us a solid clue. It's a war chariot. It will not start but end a war.

The word *melakah* means works prescribed to. Since this pattern of the chariot of the cherubim represented real heavenly things that have certain works prescribed to them, David may have even understood that God ordained the flaming sword to strike Earth when evil has come to a head at the end of our age. The Lord told Israel,

And if ye will not be reformed . . . Then will I also walk contrary unto you, and will punish you yet seven times for your sins. And **I will bring a sword upon you, that shall avenge the quarrel of my covenant.**[13]

Here the sword is mentioned in connection with the Lord's covenant. The quarrel of his covenant is serious business. Earth will be purged. The terrible catastrophe that will hit as the shortened Tribulation ends is covered in detail in my book, *Exit: 2007, The Secret of Secrets Revealed.*

Tabniyth, translated "pattern," means model, figure, resemblance, likeness, and similitude. The chariot of the cherubim is a figure that symbolizes real things in the heavens.

Patterns of Things in The Heavens

According to Hebrews 9:23,24, the tabernacle contained "patterns (*hupodeigmata*, representations) of things in the heavens . . . which are the figures (*antitupa*, counterparts) of the true." Referring to the earthly tabernacle as "the example and shadow of heavenly things," Hebrews 8:1,5; 9:11 says,

We have such an high priest (Christ), who is set on the right hand of the throne of the Majesty **in the heavens;** A minister of the sanctuary, and of **the true tabernacle, which the Lord pitched,** and not man. . . . (Earthly priests) serve unto the **example and shadow of heavenly things**. . . . But Christ (is) being come an high priest of good things to come, by a greater and more perfect tabernacle, not made with hands, that is to say, not of this building.

The Greek word translated "building" is *ktiseos* and means creation, as in Green's Interlinear Hebrew/Greek-English Bible. This creation refers to the renovation of planet Earth after it had been ruined, probably by the asteroid impact that destroyed the dinosaurs and mammoths.

Creation Week

This creation week started on Sunday, September 13, 4043 B.C. with "Let there be light" in Genesis 1:3 and ended when God rested on the equivalent of the Jewish Tishri 1, the Feast of Trumpets (our Saturday, September 19), the day after Adam and Eve were created. That is the day this *kosmos,* or present harmonious order of things, began to operate in the world. (See

Exit: 2007, The Secret of Secrets Revealed for more details.)

CREATION WEEK

September, B.C. 4043

Sun	Mon	Tues	Wed	Thu	Fri	Sat
13	14	15	16	17	18	19

Generations of Old

Both Heaven and Earth were originally formed long before this, a time simply referred to in Genesis 1:1 as "the beginning," and as Isaiah: 45:18 says, "(He) created it not in vain (*tohu,* an empty, waste, desolated surface), he formed it to be inhabited."

After the catastrophe that caused the mass extinction, the Earth became "without form (*tohu,* an empty, waste, desolated surface), and void (*bohu,* an empty, indistinguishable ruin)," as we find in Genesis 1:2. Then, in order for the Earth to be a good habitat for Adam and the animals, the Lord "renewest the face (surface) of the earth."[14]

The word translated renewest is *chadash,* repaired, restored. The Lord repaired the damage, restored the Earth to its pristine beauty, and created man and animals to inhabit it.

Our solar system was created "in the ancient (*qedem,* aforetime) days, in the generations (*dowr,* ages or revolutions of time) of old" as mentioned in Isaiah 51:9. The true tabernacle in the heavens is of that earlier creation.

A Cloud by Day, A Fire by Night

The earthly tabernacle set up by Moses was made up of two sections, the outer Holy Place and the inner Holy of Holies. In general, the outer Holy Place symbolized Israel's earthly worship of the heavenly God under the first covenant. Christ was prefigured by the shew bread and the golden candlestick. He is the true bread of life and the light of the world. This depiction of the Holy Place was largely fulfilled in the first covenant that ended in 30 A.D. with the crucifixion and resurrection of Jesus Christ.

The thick veil that hung across the doorway leading from the Holy Place into the Holy of Holies was a type of the human body of Jesus. Hebrews 10:19,20 speaks of "a new and living way, which he hath consecrated for us, through the veil, that is to say, his flesh." As his flesh was sacrificed, that heavy veil was supernaturally ripped from top to bottom, opening the way into heaven, and a new era began under a new covenant. (This is a clue that the Holy of Holies represented heaven.)

If we believe in him, we are said to be "in Christ."[15] Because God looks upon the church as being the body of Christ, his perfect sacrifice atones for our sins, and we can go to heaven to be with him where he is. He is the door by which we enter heaven.

In Exodus 25:8, the Lord said, "Let them make me a sanctuary that I may dwell among them." Therefore, the tabernacle that Moses built had to do with the Lord's dwelling place. His presence was manifested to the Israelites in the wilderness by a pillar of cloud by day and in a fire by night.

> Thou goest before them, by daytime in a pillar of a cloud, and in a pillar of fire by night.[16]

Both were visible above the tabernacle dwelling place. This was an excellent picture. Heaven is visible above Earth, and it actually does resemble a cloud by day and a fire by night.

The Work of God's Hands

In the beginning, God brought our solar system into being as part of his original creation of the universe. The heavens are said to be the work of God's hands. David said,

Of old hast thou laid the foundation of the earth: and **the heavens are the work of thy hands.**[17]

When I consider **thy heavens, the work of thy fingers,** the moon and the stars, which thou hast ordained; What is man, that thou art mindful of him?[18]

The following is probably not how God actually created the planets, but it is a figure that symbolizes that creation and helps us understand the end result. Imagine that God sat out in space on the orbit of the Earth, and pitched ten flying heavenly bodies from his fingers, five from the left hand (Mercury, Venus, Earth, Mars, and Rahab, Satan's planet that split and formed our Asteroid Belt), and five from the right hand (Jupiter, Saturn, Uranus, Neptune, and Pluto).

According to the force of the throw and the English put on each ball, some ended up in orbit nearby, others circled the sun farther away, but all wheeled around their orbits in the same direction and on nearly the same plane.

Isaiah 48:13 lends itself easily to such a picture. The Lord said,

> Mine hand (picture his left hand) also hath laid the foundation of the earth (along with the other terrestrial planets, Mercury, Venus, Mars, and Rahab), and my right hand hath spanned the heavens (including Jupiter, Saturn, Uranus, Neptune, and Pluto): when I call unto them they stand up (*amad,* are established) together.

Since the planets are said to stand up together, it looks like our entire solar system was established at the same time.

THE TEN ORIGINAL CHERUBIM

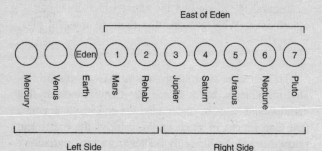

Originally, seven cherubim, or planets, seem to have been placed to the east of Eden. Remember the divisions, five on the left, five on the right and seven to the east of Eden. They will tie in with the tabernacle and its furnishings later on.

Split by a Stone

The planet Rahab that was originally assigned to Satan was split to pieces during ancient times, that is, before Adam's day. A stray stone must have been hurled at it because of the sins of Satan (also called the Devil, dragon, and serpent[19]) and his fallen angels called demons. Mars was peppered with stones as a result of the tremendous explosion. This is why one side of Mars has more craters than the other side.

Some pieces of Rahab were thrown out into cometary orbits. Some of them cross or come near to Earth's orbit. They have been called Earth crossers, Earth grazers and even Earth smashers because the potential for destruction is there.

A piece of that planet probably did hit Earth at something like 40,000 miles per hour and destroyed the dinosaurs. Scientists think they have located the crater left by the impact of a six-mile-wide asteroid[20] at the edge of the Yucatan Peninsula. Chicxulub Crater is 185 miles in diameter.[21]

That explosion blanketed the world with a thin clay layer containing an iridium anomaly, an unusually high amount. This much iridium is only found in the core of the Earth or in extraterrestrial objects. Another impact explosion will happen at the end of the Tribulation, a time so terrible that it has to be shortened or no flesh would be saved.[22]

Small pieces of the shattered planet hit Earth from time to time, about 40,000 tons annually. Most of these meteors burn up in our atmosphere. If large enough to survive their fiery entry, they are called meteorites.

Some are iron from the core of the planet. Others are stone. The carbonaceous chondrites are water-soluble, clay-like stones. It's obvious that the source planet was a terrestrial planet similar to our own.

Two very large carbonaceous chondrite meteorites, the 800-pound Murchison and the one-ton Allende, hit Earth in 1969. The former fell in February; the latter fell in September. Both of them contain amino acids, the basic building blocks of life, and interesting minerals such as diamonds, silicon carbide, graphite, titanium carbide and aluminum oxide.[23]

Earth Spared Break-up

Revelation 8:10 shows that a "star" (*aster*) will impact Earth when the third trumpet sounds, but unlike Satan's planet Rahab, Earth will not split into pieces. It will be badly scarred but not wiped out. It has been established for ever.

> And he built his sanctuary like high palaces, like **the earth which he hath established for ever.**[24]

When necessary, it will be renewed, and there will always be an Earth.

When John said, "I saw a new heaven and a new earth: for the first heaven and the first earth were passed away,"[25] the word translated new is *kainon*. It also means recently made fresh or unworn. Where Revelation 21:5 has, "I make all things new," Thayer's Lexicon translates it as "I bring all things into a new and better condition" and says *kainos* is used to denote "the new, primarily in reference to quality, the fresh, unworn."

The word translated "passed away" is *parerchomai*.

Thayer's lists the meaning as "to go past," also "to be carried past." There will come a time when these two planets will have gone past their prime and will therefore be renovated.

When the asteroid hits Earth at an oblique angle, this sphere will turn upside down, but the Lord will hold its supports firm.

> BEHOLD, the LORD maketh the earth empty, and maketh it waste, and **turneth it upside down,** and scattereth abroad the inhabitants . . . The land shall be utterly emptied, and utterly spoiled . . . because they have transgressed the laws, changed the ordinance, broken the everlasting covenant. Therefore hath the curse (the asteroid) devoured the earth . . . the inhabitants of the earth are **burned, and few men left.**[26]

> When the earth and all its people quake, it is I who hold its pillars (supports) firm. Selah.[27]

When you see the word "Selah," it means just pause and think of that. It is used in Scripture to call your attention to something important. No matter what the Earth goes through, it will not explode into pieces like Rahab.

Whether this planet will right itself completely is not clear. It will settle down and regain its equilibrium, but it seems possible that it could swap north pole for south pole. The tilt of our axis could change. It could come out of it with reversed magnetic polarity. The magnetic record in our seabeds shows that the polarity has reversed several times in the past. An oblique hit by an asteroid might trigger a reversal.

Rahab Shattered

It looks like the asteroid will crash into Earth because of a whirlwind sent by the Lord. This was probably true in the case of the planet Rahab also, because Job says that the heavens are cleared by his breath. This is the way evil is done away with. Isaiah 26:21; 27:1 says that the Lord cometh

> out of **his place** (heaven) to punish the inhabitants of the earth for their iniquity . . . IN that day the LORD with his sore and great and strong **sword** (the 'flaming sword') shall punish leviathan the piercing serpent, even leviathan that crooked serpent; and he shall slay the dragon that is in the sea (nations[28]).

Leviathan the piercing serpent represents the Satan-possessed False Prophet. Satan pierces and enters his body, taking it over and using it as his own. Leviathan that crooked serpent is the Satan-obsessed Beast of Rome. Satan controls him from without. The dragon that is in the nations is Satan himself. Some have dubbed these three the Satanic trinity.

Rahab is a good name for Satan's planet because that name is associated with the harlot of Jericho.[29] Rahab also means proud, and Satan's sin was because of his pride. Concerning the planet, Scripture says,

> And by His understanding **He shattered Rahab. By His breath** (*ruwach,* spirit, breath, wind) **the heavens are cleared;** His hand has pierced the fleeing serpent (Satan).[30]

Thou hast broken Rahab in pieces, as one that is slain: thou hast scattered thine enemies (Satan and his fallen angels) with thy strong arm.[31]

Awake, awake, put on strength, O arm of the LORD (Jesus Christ[32]); awake, as in the ancient days, in the generations of old. **Art thou not it that hath cut** (*chatsab,* **split,** as a stone-cutter) **Rahab,** and wounded the dragon (Satan)?[33]

Some astronomers think that there was a planet where our Asteroid Belt is at the present time. Others think that the planetesimals that would have formed a planet under ordinary circumstances were prevented from doing so because of perturbations by the nearby giant, Jupiter. They should consider what the Scripture says. Rahab was obviously whole at one time and later became broken.

Ten Curtains, Ten Cherubim
The Lord built the tabernacle like the planets in the heavens, which are like planet Earth. Psalms 78:69 says,

And he built his sanctuary like high palaces (*ruwm,* 'high places of heaven'[34]), **like the earth which he hath established for ever.**

The word translated sanctuary is *miqdash.* Gesenius' Lexicon says it is "specially used of the holy tabernacle."[35]

The ten original planets in our solar system were represented by the ten curtains that covered the tabernacle. That is why cherubim were embroidered on them. Moses was instructed to

> make the tabernacle with **ten curtains** of fine twined linen, and blue, and purple, and scarlet: **with cherubims** of cunning work shalt thou make them.[36]

Isaiah 40:22 uses figurative language. The heavens are "as a curtain" and "as a tent," and the Lord dwells in this tent. It is God

> that sitteth upon the circle (*chuwg,* circuit, i.e., orbit) of the earth . . . that stretcheth out **the heavens as a curtain,** and spreadeth them out **as a tent to dwell in.**

This verse is why I said to imagine that God was sitting out on the orbit of the Earth when he pitched the planets from his ten fingers.

The curtain was made of ten widths of fabric, each embroidered with cherubim. Two panels consisting of five widths each were sewn together. Then both sets of five were also coupled together. Moses was told to fasten the pair together with loops and taches (knobs or clasps) of gold "and it shall be one tabernacle."[37]

The whole tabernacle curtain represents our entire planetary solar system. As if flung from God's left hand, five of the widths represent the terrestrial planets Mercury, Venus, Earth, Mars and Satan's planet Rahab. As if flung from his right hand, the other five widths represent the four giant planets, Jupiter, Saturn, Uranus, and Neptune plus tiny Pluto.

Even the clasps and loops fastening both five-width

panels together fit into the picture. They suggest the orbits and rocks of the Asteroid Belt after Satan's planet Rahab was split by a stray rock. Most of the asteroids are between the inner and outer planets, between Mars and the giant planet Jupiter.

God dwells inside the perimeter of the heavenly tent, and therefore within our solar system boundaries. He dwells on a planet, not the sun. He does not dwell on Mercury or Pluto either, for he "dwellest between the cherubims."[38] Therefore, he does not dwell on either of the outside planets.

A Blueprint

Concerning the earthly tabernacle set up by Moses, Exodus 25:8,9 in the Jerusalem Bible says,

> Make me a sanctuary (*miqdash*, tabernacle) so that I can reside among them. You will make it all according to the design for the **Dwelling** and the design for its furnishings which I shall now show you.

In the King James Version, instead of the word "design," the translators used the word "pattern." This ties in with the description in Hebrews 8:5, which mentions "the pattern shewed to thee (Moses) in the mount." The tabernacle was a pattern of heavenly things.

This design seems to be a blueprint of heavenly things, reduced in scale and drawn with many symbols. Just as an architect must know what the symbols he uses represent, we must figure out what these symbols represent to read this blueprint.

The Lord's Dwelling Place

The earthy tabernacle was the dwelling place of the Lord, and the heavenly realities it represented include the Lord's residence. It is in the same definite **place** Jesus was referring to in John 14:2:

> In my Father's house are many mansions: if it were not so, I would have told you. I go to prepare a place (*topon,* an area that is **marked off** from the surrounding space) for you.

I can't explain it yet, but tack this back there in your mind somewhere. Remember that this place is marked off from the surrounding space. You will find out how it is literally marked off later.

As explained in detail on pages 209–211 in *Exit: 2007, The Secret of Secrets Revealed,* the cherubim are symbols of all ten of the original planets.

Ezekiel's Visions of The Cherubim

The orbits of just four of the cherubim form the wheels within wheels Ezekiel saw around the blazing sun in his visions when **"the heavens were opened"** to him in Ezekiel, chapter one.

The flying heavenly bodies themselves looked to him "like burning coals of fire." Verse 13 is translated clearly in the New Scofield Bible:

> As for the likeness of the living creatures, their appearance was **like burning coals of fire.**

Looking up at the sky, Ezekiel saw a whirling wind come out of the north and form a great doughnut-shaped cloud representing our asteroid belt. In the center of that orbiting cloud was a bright amber hub, our radiant sun. Verse 4 describes the sun as "a fire infolding itself, and a brightness (*nogah*, **sunlight**) was about it."

Finding out that this brightness was literally sunlight helped me to understand what this represented. Our sun is a fire infolding itself. It is an atomic furnace. Viewing the sun during an eclipse with our big telescopes, flames can be seen leaping up and curving back down into the ball of fire.

None of these four cherubim are the Lord's throne. His throne is above them.

In the space between the central sun and the asteroid belt Ezekiel saw four flying heavenly bodies whose complete orbits formed four high concentric rings, or full orbs, around the sun. According to verse 16, "their appearance and their work was as it were (symbolic language) **a wheel in the middle of a wheel**."

When you see "like" or "as," it is symbolic or figurative language. Here, it tells us that these are not real wheels, they just look like wheels. The word for wheel in the original is *owphan*, to revolve. These wheels are the revolves, or orbits, of the four heavenly bodies that Ezekiel called cherubim.

Hammer of Earth

Among the planets, Ezekiel saw something else. He said that "it went up and down among the living creatures (verse 13). It is an asteroid with a cometary orbit—doomsday rock. Reading different translations of verse 13 helps us get a better picture of this rock. It resembles a torch as it orbits among the cherubim just as asteroids show up as streaks against the stationary stars on the astronomer's photograph.

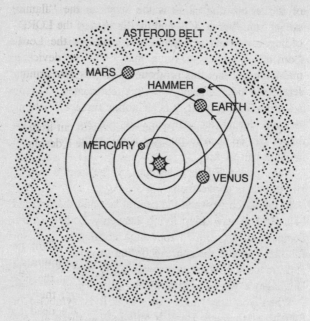

Four cherubim, Mercury, Venus, Earth and Mars

In the midst of the living beings there was something that looked like burning coals of fire, like torches darting back and forth among the living beings (lively things). The fire was bright, and lightning was flashing from the fire (NASB).

The appearance of the living creatures was like burning coals of fire or like torches. Fire moved back and forth among the creatures; it was bright, and lightning flashed out of it (NIV).

This stone that will hit Earth is called "the hammer

of the whole earth.'' It is the same as the ''flaming sword'' of Genesis 3:24 and the ''sword of the LORD'' of Jeremiah 47:6. Jeremiah also called it the Lord's ''device.'' Instead of being man's nuclear device as many think, this device is from the Lord's own armory. Jeremiah said.

> How is **the hammer** of the whole earth cut asunder and broken! how is Babylon become a desolation among the nations![39]

The Hebrew word *gada* is translated ''cut asunder.'' It means cut off. *Shabar,* translated ''broken,'' also means split in pieces. The asteroid hammer that will pound Earth at Babylon is a piece that was split off of the planet Rahab. It is **the stone ''cut out of the mountain without hands''** that the Lord will throw at the final evil world empire to break it to pieces. After the wind carries the dust away (and Israel buries the dead for seven Jewish months[40]) the Rock that is Christ will set up his kingdom and rule over the whole Earth.[41]

> The LORD hath opened **his armoury,** and hath brought forth the weapons of his indignation: for this is the work of the Lord GOD of hosts in the land of the Chaldeans (Babylon).[42]

> For this is the day of the Lord GOD of hosts, a day of vengeance, that he may avenge him of his adversaries: and **the sword** shall devour, and it shall be satiate and made drunk with their blood: for the Lord GOD of hosts hath a sacrifice . . . by the river Euphrates.''[43]

His device is against Babylon, to destroy it (Jeremiah 51:11).

The Strange Act

The strike of the Sword of the Lord is the Lord's "strange work," his "strange act." Isaiah 28:21 explains,

> For the LORD shall rise up as in mount Perazim, he shall be wroth as in the valley of Gibeon (Joshua's long day, when more died with the great stones cast down by the Lord than Israel killed[44]), that he may do **his work, his strange work;** and bring to pass **his act, his strange act.**

Ezekiel's Visions Unlocked

Translators have had a hard time with Ezekiel's visions in chapters one and ten. It always helps to have some idea of what the text is trying to say. In this case, they obviously didn't have a clue as to what the cherubim really represented.

Verse 17 in the Concordant Literal Bible best reveals their circular orbits: "When they go, toward one of their four quarters are they going." To picture this, imagine our orange again with its rind scored into four quarters. The only way to travel toward each quarter in turn is to go in a full circle.

After finding that the word translated brightness in Ezekiel 1:4 really meant sunlight, I began to get a glimmer of what Ezekiel's mysterious vision described. Then the meaning was finally unlocked for me by the key phrase in Ezekiel 1:15:

Now as I beheld the living creatures, behold **one wheel upon the earth.**

Ezekiel 10:9 says that one wheel is by one cherub, and another wheel is by another cherub. Therefore, if each of the four cherubim have one wheel apiece, and one wheel is upon the Earth, the Earth is one of the flying heavenly bodies. Its wheel, or revolve, is its orbit.

One is the Earth, their "appearance was like burning coals of fire," and according to verse 16, all "four had one likeness." Yet, verse 5 says, "And this was their appearance; they had the likeness of a man." The translation of the word *adam* as "man" obscured the true meaning here.

The word *adam* means man, as being ruddy, but it basically means red earth, and that is what is referred to here. Adam was given this name because his body was formed from red clay.

In addition to the red clay located in many different places upon the continents, fine red clay is found in the depths of our Pacific Ocean. Endlessly circulating in the oceanic mixing bowl, this rock flour, eroded from all continents, represents an average of the mineral makeup of the entire surface of this planet. Therefore, it is no big surprise to find the Earth characterized as being covered with red earth.

The four planets seen by Ezekiel all look like burning coals of fire when reflecting the sunlight, but they actually have red earth or clay soil on all four quarters. They are the terrestrial planets Mercury, Venus, Earth, and Mars. They are also called the inner planets because they are close to the sun.

Surely most of you have seen Venus. If you have ever looked up at the stars and picked out one that looked bigger and brighter than all the rest, it probably was Venus. Next to the sun and moon, it is the brightest thing in the sky. There are even times when it can be seen after dawn in the daylight near the ascending sun.

Knowing that the cherubim are planets makes Ezekiel 1:7 come clear. It says,

> And their feet (extremities, limbs; astronomers call the edge of a celestial disk its limb) were straight (*yashar*, smooth) feet (edges); and the sole (*kaph*, curve) of their feet (edges) was like the sole of a calf's foot (round): and they sparkled like the colour of burnished brass.

In other words, the curve of their limb, outer edges, looked smooth and round. All the planets Ezekiel saw are round and sparkle in the sunlight.

You can see why I had to look up the meanings of most of the words in the original language to find out what this was talking about. The next verse says that the planets have

> the hands (*yad*, parts, i.e., elements) of a man (*adam*, red earth) under (*tachath*, used of things which are interchanged, in lieu of, instead of) their wings (*kanaph*, quarters) on their four sides (*reba*, fourth parts).[45]

All that the above complicated passage means is that each sphere has elements of clay soil on all quarters. It wouldn't have been so complicated if the translators had understood what it was talking about.

As mentioned before, Green's Interlinear Hebrew Greek-English Bible mentions the "four wings of the earth'' in Isaiah 11:12, and Ezekiel 1:6 says of the cherubim, ''every one had four wings.'' We have seen photographs of Earth from space and know that it has no wings.

Again, we have symbolic language. The planets fly, but these are not actually wings but *kanaph,* quarters. The four wings are the four quarters of each orb, or sphere.

Two of the quarters are joined together covering half the body, and two are joined together covering the other half as on our orange with its rind scored in quarters. Concerning the wings of the cherubim, Scripture says that

> every one had two, which covered on this side, and every one had two, which covered on that side, their bodies (Ezekiel 1:23).

EARTH'S "WINGS" SUGGEST HER ASTRONOMICAL SYMBOL, ⊕

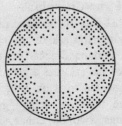

The planets are said to raise up their wings to symbolize flight. They actually are zipping around in space at a very fast clip. Earth is travelling 18.51 miles per second. The following table shows how fast each of the planets that you can see with the unaided eye travel. Saturn is the slow planet.

AVERAGE ORBITAL VELOCITY
OF THE NAKED-EYE PLANETS

	miles per second
Mercury	29.76
Venus	21.77
Mars	14.99
Jupiter	8.52
Saturn	5.99

In 3000 B.C., the Sumerians listed ten planets, but western astronomers only knew of six, Mercury, Venus, Earth, Mars, Jupiter, and Saturn, until 1781 when Uranus was discovered. Neptune was found in 1846. Pluto was not located until 1930. Only since 1930 has it been possible for us to figure out that the ten curtains represented the original ten planets in our solar system.

The Chariot of The Cherubim

In the innermost part of the Tabernacle was a rectangular chest called the ark of the covenant. Inside it were the ten commandments on two "tables of stone." On top of the ark was a golden lid called the mercy seat. Connected to it on either side were two winged cherubim made of beaten gold. Protruding through four rings, two on either side of the ark, were two shafts for carrying it that were never to be removed, but were drawn out far enough for their ends to be seen from the Holy Place. To be seen from the Holy Place, it seems that they would have had to stick out under the hangings.

And they drew out the staves, that the ends of the staves were seen out in the holy place before the oracle.[46]

Keep the cherubim flanking the ark with its mercy seat and the two shafts in your mind. Use your imagination. You are trying to figure out what the chariot of the cherubim is.

To get a mental picture of the chariot of the cherubim instead of thinking of these two cherubim as winged creatures similar to pictures of angels, substitute some of the heavenly reality for the symbolic figures. A different image will emerge.

The two cherubim are two planets, each with its own orbit or wheel. In your mind, stand the wheels on their edges as if ready to carry a carriage down a path. Next, imagine one wheel at each side of the mercy seat covering the ark and the two shafts protruding from the rings on the side of the ark at a downward angle so their ends can be seen sticking out from under the hangings between the Holy of Holies and the Holy Place.[47] There is your chariot, with its two shafts, its seat, a storage compartment underneath the seat containing two stone tablets, and its two wheels.

What its parts depict orbit in the heavens. Hebrews 9:5 in Green's Interlinear Bible says that above the ark were "the cherubim of glory over-shadowing the mercyseat (of which we cannot now speak part by part)." The KJV has, "And over it the cherubims of glory shadowing the mercyseat; of which we cannot now speak particularly." The Lamsa version is clearer: "And over it the cherubim of glory, overshadowing the mercy seat; now is not the time to describe how these things were made."

The Time of The End

These things were not meant to be completely understood until the time of the end began in 1967, when Israel grew four leaves, the Gaza Strip, the Golan Heights, the Sinai, and the West Bank, fulfilling the fig tree parable of Matthew 24:32–34, According to that parable, Christ and the kingdom of God were to be "near, even at the doors," when young Israel "putteth forth leaves."

In 1967, Israel took the rest of Jerusalem, which also ended the times of the Gentiles. Luke 21:24 showed that the Jews would be taken into captivity and ended by saying,

Jerusalem shall be trodden down of the Gentiles,
until the times of the Gentiles be fulfilled.

Israel is now not only back in the land but has control of Jerusalem and the temple area. The prophesied end time events are now dead ahead. When the Israelites came out of Egypt, the nineteen year old boys were not counted. After wandering in the wilderness 40 years while the older generation, except Joshua and Caleb, died off, they went into the promised land.

This was a type that we are seeing repeated today, and remember, history does repeat itself. Job 11:6 says that

the secrets of wisdom . . . are double to that which is!

There are many types and dramatizations the Lord had played out to help us understand prophecy. History repeats itself because the Lord planned it that way. Israel was nineteen when the Six-Day War took place. Forty more years and they will again be gathered in their promised land. Twenty-seven of those years are already behind us. Truly, Christ "is near, even at the doors."[48]

Two Doors

There are two doors. When heaven's door opens, the Rapture will take place. The other door is Rapture II. It will open in the 40th year. The Tribulation saints will be "saved: yet so as by fire,"[49] just as Lot barely made it out of Sodom before it was destroyed by fire.

Peace, Peace, When There is No Peace

Israel has already started the process of making peace with the PLO and the Arab countries. It started with Egypt. Israel has now turned over Gaza and Jericho to the Palestinians. The Washington Declaration, initialed July 25, 1994, between Israel and Jordan ended the war between those two countries. Air flights are now scheduled between them, and people can cross the border between the two countries easier. Diplomatic overtures are even being made between Syria and Israel.

A Vatican-Israeli accord is near. The Orange County Register of May 26, 1994, reported that the Vatican is drafting a document that acknowledges that the church fostered centuries of anti-Semitism in a "mind-boggling" draft intended to improve relations with Israel. "The negotiations are to resolve long-standing disputes holding up full diplomatic relations between the Vatican and Israel."

The 17th Pentecostal World Conference is to meet in Jerusalem in September, 1995. The Vatican faithful will be there. Also, the Pope is planning to visit Iraq, and the headquarters of the world church will be moved to Babylon during the Tribulation.[50]

On his planned visit to the United States, it is reported that **the Pope will speak at the General Assembly of the United Nations on the subject of world peace.**

I don't know how anyone can help but see what this is leading to. The stage is being set. We are seeing the preliminaries already taking place.

This will all culminate in the signing of a seven-year peace treaty by two men, a leader in Rome, who at that time will be head of both the world church and the world government,[51] and the leader of Israel on the Feast of Weeks in 2001, kicking off the Tribulation, called the Seventieth Week of Daniel. Sivan 6 will fall on Monday, May 28, in 2001. (See *Exit: 2007, The Secret of Secrets Revealed* for more details and the dates of all important end-time events.)

Time For Hidden Things to Come to Light

We are near the end. The time is right to increase our knowledge of Bible prophecy. It is the time when all the hidden things can come to light, when the church is old and ready for her strong meat.

> But strong meat belongeth to them that are of full age, even those who by reason of use have their senses exercised to discern both good and evil.[52]

We were meant to understand these things in the latter days after the time of the end began. Jeremiah 30:23,24 says,

Behold, the whirlwind of the LORD goeth forth with fury, a continuing (*garar,* destroying) whirlwind: it shall fall with pain upon the head of the wicked (the False Prophet). The fierce anger of the LORD shall not return, until he have done it, and until he have performed the intents of his heart: **in the latter days** (now) **ye shall consider** (*biyn,* **understand**) **it.**

Another passage that says that we will understand this in the latter days is found in Jeremiah 23:18–20. I would be afraid to say that this passage refers to me, but the similarities make me wonder if it could be possible. I stand fast and have no doubts whatsoever. I have heard the Lord speak to me and say, ''Be still and know that I am God,'' and I have certainly marked his word. He has opened my understanding and has shown me what the whirlwind will toss into the Earth. Whatever else it means, it shows that we are to understand in the latter days. Jeremiah said,

For who hath stood (*amad,* continued to stand fast) in the counsel (*cowd,* inward secret counsel) of the LORD, and hath perceived and heard his word? who hath marked his word, and heard it? Behold, a whirlwind of the LORD is gone forth in fury, even a grievous whirlwind: it shall fall grievously upon the head of the wicked. The anger of the LORD shall not return, until he have executed, and till he have performed the thoughts of his heart: **in the latter days ye shall consider** (*biyn,* **understand**) **it perfectly** (Jeremiah 23:18–20).

In the Septuagint, Jeremiah 37:23 says, "For the wrathful anger of the Lord has gone forth . . . **in the latter days ye shall know these things.**"

We are living in the latter days. The time of the end began when Israel took Jerusalem, ending the Times of the Gentiles.[53] It is now time for all the deep things to surface.

Chariot of Fire

When Elijah was taken up to heaven by a whirlwind, it was a type of the Rapture. We will probably be taken up by a whirlwind too. I imagine it will be like being whooshed up a giant air tube.

Just as Elijah was taken up before his successor Elisha died, the Rapture will take place some time before the flaming sword hits. When Elijah went up, a chariot of fire became visible. In II Kings 2:11,12 says that there

> appeared a chariot of fire, and horses of fire, and parted them both asunder; and Elijah went up by a whirlwind into heaven. And Elisha saw it, and he cried, My father, My father, **the chariot of Israel,** and the horsemen (driver, in the Confraternity version) thereof.

This chariot has something to do with the Lord's destroying weapon, called the flaming sword, the sword of the Lord, and the arrow of the Lord's deliverance. In II Kings 13:14–17, when

> Elisha was fallen sick of his sickness whereof he died. . . . Joash the king of Israel . . . said, O my father, my father, **the chariot of Israel,** and the

horsemen (guider, Confraternity) thereof. And Elisha said unto him, Take bow and arrows . . . Elisha put his hands upon the king's hands. And he said, Open the window **eastward**. . . . Then Elisha said, **Shoot.** And he shot. And he said, **The arrow of the LORD'S deliverance.**

The Lord is the driver of the chariot in the heavenly tabernacle. At the end of the age, Israel will be attacked by a multinational army and the Lord will come to their defense.[54]

Eastward reminds us that a hail of stones and coals of fire will fall when the asteroid, "the arrow of the Lord's deliverance," is shot toward a land **east** of Israel. It will land at Babylon on the Euphrates in Iraq. Psalms 18:10–13 says,

He rode upon a cherub, and did fly: yea, he did fly upon the wings (*kanaph*, quarters) of the wind (i.e., he orbited). He made darkness **his secret place;** his pavilion (*cukkah*, tent, tabernacle) round about him were dark waters and thick clouds of the skies. At the brightness that was before him his thick clouds passed, hail stones and **coals of fire.**

Our Mercy Seat

Christ is more than just the driver of the chariot, he is positioned there as our mercy seat.

All have sinned and come short of the glory of God, being justified as a free gift, by His grace, through the redemption which is in Christ Jesus.

For God has set Him out **as a mercy seat** (*hilasterion*, mercy seat, propitiation) through faith in His blood.[55]

He is the propitiation (the atoning sacrifice) for our sins: and not for our's only, but also for the sins of the whole world (for there is no other Saviour).[56]

If we accept Jesus Christ as our Saviour, his blood that was shed for us atones for our sins. His sacrifice applies to us, and we can enter heaven's door. If we try to get in by any other route, "sin lieth at the door." Romans 6:23 is very clear,

"For the wages of sin is death: but the gift of God is eternal life through Jesus Christ our Lord."

Acts 4:12 adds a very important warning. It says,

Neither is there salvation in any other: for there is none other name (than Jesus) under heaven given among men, whereby we must be saved.

Mysteries Solved

We have already learned that the cherubim are planets and that there are at least two between Earth and heaven. The flaming sword is a split piece of the planet Rahab that was probably blasted asunder because of Satan's sin. This asteroid stands guard duty to prevent the evil that spread over Earth from infecting heaven. The chariot of the cherubim is a war chariot about to dump its bomb on Babylon. We have also found out that the ten curtains in the tabernacle represent ten cherubim, or planets, in our solar system.

While solving the mystery of the chariot of the cherubim, we have discovered some more clues that help us identify heaven.

Clues

Between us and Heaven are at least two planets (Gen. 3:24). The Tabernacle symbolizes the heavens (Heb. 9:23–24). The ten Tabernacle curtains represent ten planets (Ex. 26:1). Heaven is marked off from the surrounding space.

3 ✣ The Vengeance of His Temple

THERE IS A PAY-BACK. NO MATTER HOW BADLY this world treats us, we can take heart, for the Lord has promised that he will take vengeance in our stead for wrongs done to us. In Romans 12:17–19, Paul made this very clear when he said,

Recompense to no man evil for evil. Provide things honest in the sight of all men. If it be possible, as much as lieth in you, live peaceably with all men. Dearly beloved, avenge not yourselves, but rather give place unto wrath: for it is written, Vengeance is mine; I will repay, saith the Lord.

The book of Revelation is like a drama played out for us just before the Rapture takes place. After we are in heaven, the things from chapter 4:1 on will actually begin to happen.

When we hear the souls under the altar cry out, "How long, O Lord, holy and true, dost thou not judge and avenge our blood on them that dwell on the earth,[1] a big pay-back is not far away. Just before the Lord's vengeance is to be cast upon the Earth, incense is offered "with the prayers of all saints upon the golden altar which (is) before the throne."[2] When that happens, it is certain that those prayers are about to be answered.

Something in the tabernacle and later in the temple, symbolized this vengeance of the Lord. In Scripture, the "arrow of the LORD's deliverance" and some "coals of fire" refer to the Lord's device that administers the vengeance of his temple. It will land east of Jerusalem at Babylon. Jeremiah 51:11 says,

> His device is against Babylon, to destroy it; because it is the vengeance of the LORD, **the vengeance of his temple.**

This is the literal city of Babylon on the Euphrates River in Iraq. Saddam Hussain has been rebuilding it on the original site about 62 miles south of Baghdad. Work on it was going on even during the war between Iran and Iraq.

Saddam held the first annual Babylon International Festival from September 22 to October 22, in 1987. At that time, posters announced,

FROM NABUKHADNEZZAR TO SADDAM HUSSEIN
BABYLON UNDERGOES A RENAISSANCE

Another in this series of festivals was held in September, 1992. The rebuilding goes on.

Saddam aims to make Babylon a world-class city,

and the Bible shows that it will be. However, on the Feast of Trumpets, September 13, 2007, it will be destroyed in one hour on the first day of the Millennium. (For details on how to figure the date, see *Exit: 2007, The Secret of Secrets Revealed.*)

In The Latter Days, You Shall Understand Perfectly

We were meant to understand the Lord's vengeance in the latter days. Jeremiah 23: 18–20 says,

> Behold, a whirlwind of the LORD is gone forth in fury, even a grievous whirlwind: it shall fall grievously upon the head of the wicked. The anger of the LORD shall not return, until he have executed, and till he have performed the thoughts of his heart: **in the latter days ye shall consider** (*biyn,* **understand**) **it perfectly.**

In the Septuagint, Jeremiah 37:23 says, "For the wrathful anger of the Lord has gone forth . . . **in the latter days ye shall know these things.**" We are living in the latter days. The time of the end began with the Six-Day War in 1967. It is time for the deep things to surface.

When The Bible Says Flee, Flee

In 70 A.D., many Jews were able to escape the destruction of Jerusalem because they paid attention to the instructions found in Scripture. Concerning our days, the Lord has said.

> **Flee** out of the midst of Babylon, and deliver every man his soul: be not cut off in her iniquity;

for **this is the time of the LORD'S
vengeance** . . . Babylon is suddenly fallen and
destroyed . . . We would have healed Babylon,
but she is not healed: forsake her . . . **go every
one into his own country:** for her judgment
reacheth unto heaven, and is lifted up even to
the skies.[3]

Look at this scripture carefully. It says for everyone
to flee and go to his own country. This is because the
headquarters of the world government and the headquarters of the world church will be built in literal
Babylon on the Euphrates River in what is now Iraq.
Delegates from all nations will have their offices there.

Saddam Hussain has already rebuilt Nebuchadnez-
zars' palace,[4] and much more, but destruction cometh.
If you have offices there at the end of the shortened
Tribulation in 2007, the scriptures tell you what to do.
If you don't act on it, you will probably die in the fiery
holocaust; it is that simple. The Bible says,

Come out of her, my people, that ye be not partakers of her sins, and that ye receive not of her
plagues. For her sins have reached unto heav-
en . . . she shall be utterly burned with fire: for
strong is the Lord God who judgeth her.[5]

As Babylon hath caused the slain of Israel to fall,
so at Babylon shall fall the slain of (from) all
the earth.[6]

And the kings of the earth, who have committed
fornication (joined up with her) and lived deli-
ciously with her, shall bewail her, and lament for

her, when they shall see the smoke of her burning.
Standing afar off for the fear of her torment, saying,
Alas, alas, that great city Babylon, that mighty city!
for in one hour is thy judgment come.[7]

Babylon—No More

The "flaming sword (*chereb*, destroying weapon)
which turned every way," is still rotating and orbiting
in the skies at the present time. It is the asteroid that
Satan has lived on since his planet Rahab was split into
pieces, and it will destroy the newly rebuilt city of
Babylon immediately after this age ends. Revelation
18:21 demonstrates this graphically:

And a mighty angel took up a **stone** like a great
millstone, and cast it into the sea, saying, Thus
with violence shall that great city Babylon be
thrown down, and shall be found no more.

The damage will be terrible and widespread. With
a worldwide earthquake, the dead will lay around the
entire world.

And the slain of the LORD shall be at that day
from one end of the earth even unto the other
end of the earth.[8]

Every wall will fall.[9] Mountains will become plains.
Even the cities of the nations will fall. These days will
be the worst since Adam was placed on Earth.

And . . . there was a great earthquake, such as
was not since men were upon the earth, so mighty

an earthquake, and so great. And the great city (Jerusalem) was divided into three parts, and **the cities of the nations fell:** and great Babylon came in remembrance before God, to give unto her the cup of the wine of the fierceness of his wrath. And every island fled away, and the mountains were not found. And there fell upon men a great hail out of heaven, every stone (rock, not ice) about the weight of a talent (about 100 pounds).[10]

The worst damage will be in an area stretching from the Euphrates River to the Nile River.

And it shall come to pass in that day, that the LORD shall beat off (*chabat,* thresh) from the channel of the river (the Euphrates) unto the stream of Egypt (the Nile).[11]

And I will make the land of Egypt desolate in the midst of the countries that are desolate, and her cities among the cities that are laid waste shall be desolate forty years.[12]

Commandments, Written in Stone

The ten commandments were not incised into stone tablets for nothing. In the end of this age, another idol will be made and placed in the temple even though the commandments include, **"Thou shalt not make unto thee any graven image"** (Exodus 20:4).

Remember how Moses smashed the original stone tablets on the ground in a flash of anger because the Israelites made the golden calf while he was on Mount Sinai? Immediately after this age ends, those who do not believe in Jesus and do not obey the commandments on those tablets will be stoned.

The Missing Commandment

The ten commandments have been given a new twist along the way by someone. Compare this list copied from the fly leaf of the Saint Joseph Textbook Edition of the Confraternity Version of the Holy Bible with Exodus 20:1–17, especially the first few verses.

THE TEN COMMANDMENTS

1. I am the Lord Thy God; thou shalt not have strange gods before Me.
2. Thou shalt not take the name of the Lord Thy God in Vain.
3. Remember thou keep holy the Sabbath Day.
4. Honor thy father and thy mother.
5. Thou shalt not kill.
6. Thou shalt not commit adultery.
7. Thou shalt not steal.
8. Thou shalt not bear false witness against thy neighbor.
9. Thou shalt not covet thy neighbor's wife.
10. Thou shalt not covet thy neighbor's goods.

Where is Exodus 20:4: **"Thou shalt not make unto thee any graven image"**? Exodus 20:3–5 in the Confraternity Version itself says something different from the list.

You shall not have other gods besides me. **You shall not carve idols for yourselves in the shape of anything** in the sky above or on the earth below or in the waters beneath the earth: **you**

shall not bow down before them or worship them. (Emphasis mine throughout.)

The Douay version puts it this way:

> Thou shalt not have strange gods before me. **Thou shalt not make to thyself a graven thing, nor the likeness of any thing** that is in heaven above, or in the earth beneath, nor of those things that are in the waters under the earth. **Thou shalt not adore them, nor serve them.**

Where does the quoted list of commandments have anything like what the Scripture really says about idols?

There is nothing wrong with the translations, but this list of commandments, called the Augustinian,[13] omits the prohibition for making images and splits the last commandment into two.

For comparison, here is the King James Version of Exodus 20:3,4,17.

> Thou shalt have no other gods before me. **Thou shalt not make unto thee any graven image, or any likeness** of any thing that is in heaven above, or that is in the earth beneath, or that is in the water under the earth. **Thou shalt not bow down thyself to them, nor serve them.** . . .

> Thou shalt not covet thy neighbour's house, thou shalt not covet thy neighbour's wife, nor his man-servant, nor his maidservant, nor his ox, nor his ass, nor any thing that is thy neighbour's (this seems all one commandment).

Judgment will fall because they will make another idol, totally disregarding one important term of God's covenant. However, this judgment is for the unsaved. Christ will take all true believers to heaven before the asteroid hits.

The church saints will go in the Rapture between now and the beginning of the seven-year Tribulation. The Tribulation saints will go in Rapture II just before the asteroid explodes in furious rebukes on Earth.

The Tribulation saints will be saved from the fiery furnace just as Shadrach, Meshach, and Abed-nego were. Their experience was a type of Rapture II.

> Nebuchadnezzar came near to the mouth of the burning fiery furnace, and . . . said . . . ye servants of the most high God, come forth, and . . . Shadrach, Meshach, and Abed-nego, **came forth of the midst of the fire** . . . and the king's counsellors . . . saw these men, upon whose bodies the fire had no power, nor was an hair of their head singed, neither were their coats changed, nor the smell of fire had passed on them. Then Nebuchadnezzar spake, and said, Blessed be the God of Shadrach, Meshach, and Abednego, who hath sent his angel, and delivered his servants that trusted in him.[14]

We must be careful how we build on the foundation of Jesus Christ. There are some that will be "saved; yet so as by fire."

> For other foundation can no man lay than that is laid, which is Jesus Christ. Now if any man build upon this foundation gold, silver, precious stones,

wood, hay, stubble; Every man's work shall be
made manifest: for the day shall declare it, because it shall be revealed by fire; and the fire
shall try every man's work of what sort it is. If
any man's work abide which he hath built there-
upon, he shall receive a reward. If any man's
work shall be burned, he shall suffer loss: but **he
himself shall be saved; yet so as by fire.**[15]

Because it was so important, immediately after the
Decalogue in Exodus 20, the Lord reinforced the prohibition against making gods of silver or gold:

And all the people saw the thunderings, and the
lightnings, and the noise of the **trumpet,** and the
mountain smoking . . . And the LORD said unto
Moses, Thus thou shalt say unto the children of
Israel, Ye have seen that I have talked with you
from heaven (Mount Sinai represented heaven).
**Ye shall not make with me gods of silver, nei-
ther shall ye make unto you gods of gold. An
altar of earth thou shalt make unto me, and
shalt sacrifice thereon thy burnt-offerings** (Exodus 20:18–24).

Here an altar is made of earth. It is a figure suggesting that Earth is considered an altar. After this age
ends, burnt-offerings will be sacrificed on the altar of
Earth when the asteroid hits on the Feast of Trumpets.

The Curse

In a vision, Zechariah saw this broken chunk of rock,
a flying rolling thing (turning "every way" as it rotates

and orbits), twice as wide as it is long. It is the flaming sword, the curse. He said,

> **This is the curse that is going forth** (orbiting) **over the face of the whole land** ('**earth,**' KJV): surely everyone who steals will be purged away according to the writing on one side (as if it were the stone tablet with the commandments on it), and everyone who swears will be purged away according to the writing on the other side (Zechariah 5:3, NASB).

The Lord said, "Behold, I am against thee, **O destroying mountain** . . . and I will stretch out mine hand upon thee, and **roll thee down from the rocks,** and will make thee a burnt mountain."[16] It is an irregular broken piece of Satan's planet, Rahab, that was split because of his sin of wanting to be like the Most High. Psalm 89:10 is now easy to understand.

> **Thou hast broken Rahab in pieces,** as one that is slain; thou hast scattered thine enemies (the dragon, Satan, and his fallen angels) with thy strong arm. The heavens are thine.

The asteroid is to be destroyed the same way the planet Rahab was—by collision. Remember Isaiah 51:9:

> **Awake, awake,** put on strength, O arm of the LORD (Christ[17]); awake, **as in the ancient days** (before Adam and Eve were put on Earth), in the generations of old. Art thou not it that hath cut Rahab, and wounded (*chalal,* pierced through) the dragon?"

Satan was wounded as with a sword. The counterpart in our days will be when the "flaming sword" of Genesis 3:24 will impact Earth at the end of this age and kill many people around the world. The idol shepherd, the Satan-possessed False Prophet will also be wounded. Scripture says,

(The) sword of the LORD shall devour from the one end of the land (earth) even to the other end of the land (earth): **no flesh shall have peace.**[18]

Woe to the idol shepherd that leaveth the flock (he will go to Babylon)! the sword shall be upon his arm, and upon his right eye: **his arm shall be clean dried up, and his right eye shall be utterly darkened.**[19]

When a stone crashed into Rahab, the impact blast whizzed this broken chunk of rock out into a cometary orbit that crosses Earth's pathway regularly. It probably crosses or comes very close to our orbit about twice a year as Icarus does.

Like the sword of Damocles, this glittering sword is an ever-present threat. Satan lives on this asteroid now, but look what will happen to it on day 2,300. On that last day of the shortened Tribulation, Isaiah 22:18,19 shows that the LORD will toss Satan's asteroid into a large country. It will hit Babylon, not tiny Israel, although coals of fire will be scattered over Jerusalem.

He will surely violently turn and **toss thee like a ball into a large country:** there shalt thou die, and there the chariots of thy glory (Rahab and the asteroid called Wormwood[20]) shall be the shame of thy lord's house (tabernacle) And **I will drive thee from thy station.**

The word translated station is *matstsab*. It means the spot where you stood, a military station. The asteroid will be driven out of the orbit he was placed in to guard the way to the tree of life. As in many other scriptures, two meanings are blended into one in this passage. It refers to Satan, who was to stand guard, and to his asteroid, which guards after he fails personally.

A similar message is found in Ezekiel 28:14–18. In the above, it says, "I will drive thee from thy station," but in Ezekiel 28, it says, "I will bring thee to ashes upon the earth." Speaking to Satan as the king of the rock (Tyrus means rock) the Lord said,

Thou art the anointed cherub that covereth (*cakak*, guards); and I have set thee so . . . thou hast walked up and down in the midst of the stones of fire (the planets). . . . thou hast sinned: therefore . . . I will destroy thee, O covering (*cakak*, guarding) cherub, from the midst of the stones of fire. . . . Thou hast defiled thy sanctuaries . . . therefore will I bring forth a fire from the midst of thee, it shall devour thee and I will bring thee to ashes upon the earth.

The asteroid will come from between the orbits of the planets and will strike Earth. This was symbolized in Ezekiel's second vision of the heavens:

Go in between the wheels (the orbits of the planets), **even under the cherub** (Satan), and fill thine hand with coals of fire from between the cherubims (planets), and scatter them over the city (Jerusalem). . . . Take **fire from between the wheels, from between the cherubims.**[21]

If we didn't understand what this meant when it mentioned taking fire from between the wheels, it tells us again plainly, "from between the cherubims."

Clashing Coals of Fire

At the end of this age, this asteroid and Earth will be on a collision course. In the LXX, Nahum 2:3,4 shows that these two chariots, the asteroid that Satan rides, and the Earth that we ride, will collide. Both look like coals of fire floating in the total darkness of space. By that time, Satan and the False Prophet will have taken military power away from individual nations and given it to the united world government. He will have

destroyed the arms of their power from among men, their mighty men sporting with fire: **the reins** (controls) **of their chariots shall be destroyed in the day of his preparation,** and the horsemen shall be thrown into confusion in the ways (*derek*, paths, i.e., orbits), and **the chariots shall clash together,** and shall be entangled in each other in the broad ways (in space): **their appearance is as lamps of fire.**

The key to understanding this passage is the last line, "their appearance is as lamps of fire." Both planets and asteroids look like lamps of fire in the dark sky.

The Day of Preparation

The day of his preparation is the day preceding the Feast of Trumpets when the seven trumpet judgments are to hit Earth after this age ends. Therefore the day of preparation is the very last day of this age, September 12, 2007, and the following day, the Feast of Trumpets, is the first day of the Millennium.

The word "preparation" has a double meaning. It represents the preparation day for the Feast of Trumpets. It also represents the altering of the orbits with a whirlwind so the two stones will collide on the Feast of Trumpets. This preparation is necessary to bring the crash to pass at this particular time.

Remember that the days of the Tribulation have to be shortened or no flesh would be saved?[22] Evidently, if struck by a direct hit later on, Earth would fly apart like Satan's planet Rahab did when our Asteroid Belt was formed. By causing an early strike, total annihilation of the human race can be avoided because Earth will be struck a glancing blow. Even so, we have seen that it will leave a swath of destruction from the Euphrates to the Nile.

> And it shall come to pass in that day, that the LORD shall beat off (*chabat*, thresh) from the channel of the river unto the stream of Egypt.

God's Fury Poured Out Like Fire

When a multinational army comes in from the north and attacks Israel, the Lord's fury will come up in his face. The Earth will be struck like a bell and the reverberations will be heard and felt around the world. Ezekiel 38:18–20 explains that

> **at the same time** when Gog shall come against the land of Israel, saith the Lord GOD, that my fury shall come up in my face. For in my jealousy and in the fire of my wrath have I spoken, Surely in that day there shall be a great shaking in the land of Israel; So that the fishes of the sea, and the fowls of the heaven, and the beasts of the field, and all creeping things that creep upon the earth, and all the men that are upon the face of the earth, shall shake at my presence, and the **mountains shall be thrown down.**

Nahum 1:5,6 describes the Lord's vengeance on the day of God's Wrath, when the flaming sword strikes Earth.

> The mountains quake at him, and the hills melt, and **the earth is burned** at his presence, yea, **the world, and all that dwell therein.** Who can stand before his indignation? and who can abide in the fierceness of his anger? his fury is poured out like fire, and **the rocks are thrown down by him.**

This is when the seven trumpet judgments will strike this Earth in quick succession. A great "star" (*aster*) will fall from heaven "burning **as it were a lamp**" and at least one fiery mountain-sized piece will split off and be cast into the sea,[23] causing a great tsunami that will dash the multinational army against the mountains of Israel. The Lord says,

> I will turn thee back, and leave but the sixth part of thee . . . Thou shalt fall upon the mountains of Israel.[24]

The Lord will be jealous for his land and pity his people. He said,

> I will remove far off (*rachaq,* thrust away, repel, cause to recede) from you the northern army, and will drive him into a land barren and desolate, with his face toward the east sea (the Dead Sea[25]), and his hinder part toward the utmost (*acharown,* western, i.e., the Mediterranean[26]) sea.[27]

Mission of The Chariot of The Cherubim

In the tabernacle, the chariot of the cherubim concealed the mystery of the vengeance of his temple in the stone tablets placed inside the Ark. The stone was in the Ark between the cherubim. The asteroid called Wormwood will orbit in space until God's pent up wrath is unleashed on the city of Babylon. It is as if the chariot of the cherubim orbits in space for a long time, then as the seventh millennium begins on the Feast of Trumpets, the first day of the seventh month of the Jewish sacred year, the Lord will fly a bombing run and drop the stone tablet that will destroy the rebuilt city of Babylon.

The last verse of the Old Testament ends with "lest I come and **smite the earth with a curse.**" This has something to do with the covenant the Lord made with

Israel, the terms of which are the Commandments, for Leviticus 26:25 says,

> And I will bring a sword upon you, that shall **avenge the quarrel of my covenant.**

Seven-Month Gap

The Second Advent could not take place on the Day of God's Wrath. Christ could not return in glory in the midst of the worst disaster since Adam was created. Malachi 3:1 says, "The Lord, whom ye seek, shall suddenly come to his temple." Yet, Hosea 9:4-7 shows that Christ, the bread of life will not come to the temple on the Feast of Trumpets, which is the day of destruction:

> their bread for their soul (Christ) shall **not come** into the house of the LORD . . . in the solemn day, and in the day of the feast of the LORD . . . they are gone because of destruction: Egypt shall gather them up, Memphis shall bury them . . . The days of recompence are come.

It will take seven months to bury the remains of the multinational army in the valley of Hamongog. The Lord said that the "name of the city shall be Hamonah (which means the multitude). Thus shall they cleanse the land."[28]

Christ will return in glory after they are buried.

> And seven months shall the house of Israel be burying of them, that they may cleanse the land. Yea, all the people of the land shall bury them;

and it shall be to them a renown **the day that I shall be glorified,** saith the Lord GOD.[29]

The Day of God's Wrath is the day of "thick darkness."[30] Zechariah 14:5–7 tells us that the light on the day of Christ's return is not dark.

And . . . the LORD my God shall come, and all the saints with thee. And it shall come to pass in that day, that the light shall not be clear, nor dark: But it shall be one day which shall be known to the LORD (he knows when he is coming), not day, nor night: but it shall come to pass, that at evening time it shall be light.

The Symbolism of Jericho

The crash of the flaming sword was prefigured when the Israelites orbited Jericho seven days carrying the Ark. On the seventh day, they went around the city seven times blowing their trumpets. When they shouted, the walls fell down flat, and they burned the city, just as every wall will fall and the noise be heard around the world when Babylon is obliterated by fire. One harlot and her family were saved from the holocaust at Jericho as a type of Rapture II.

She was saved because she was kind to the Israelite messengers who came to her house. She received them, hid them and sent them out another way so they would be safe.

At Jericho, the harlot's name was Rahab, intimating that the inhabitants of the planet Rahab were harlots, and they were. They were the angels that joined Satan and became demons.

The Way of Life and The Way of Death

Since the Crucifixion, mankind stands at the door of the Holy of Holies facing the Ark. If you enter with sin on your head, you will die. Set before you is the way of life and the way of death. Life and death, righteousness and judgment, are embodied in the mercy seat (standing for Christ and life) and the Ark (*aron, coffin,* i.e., death). Which do you choose?

After the asteroid impact, things will be different. Jeremiah 3:16,17 says that

> in those days, saith the LORD, **they shall say no more, The ark of the covenant of the LORD:** neither shall it come to mind: neither shall they remember it; neither shall they visit it; neither shall that be done any more. At that time they shall call Jerusalem the throne of the LORD and all the nations shall be gathered unto it, to the name of the LORD, to Jerusalem: **neither shall they walk any more after the imagination of their evil heart.**[31]

The Search for NEA's

Since around 20 pieces of the comet Shoemaker-Levy 9 exploded in Jupiter's atmosphere in July 1994, astronomers have been expanding their search for Near Earth Asteroids. They say they are a greater threat to Earth than wayward comets. They have identified 310 asteroids that either already cross Earth's orbit or could cross it in the future. This is an enormous threat to us. Eleanor Helin, a Jet Propulsion Laboratory planetary scientist, says, **"Earth is embedded in a swarm of asteroids."**

Asteroid impact has happened before and can happen again. There are at least 100 major craters on Earth. The biggest known to scientists is Mexico's Chicxulub Crater, thought to have been caused by an asteroid six miles across about 65,000 years ago. This is the one many think killed the dinosaurs.

Astronomers say that about eight small asteroids explode with the power of an atomic bomb in our atmosphere every year. They also think a Mars-sized rock grazed the Earth when the moon was born of the Earth.

There are various proposals for deflecting or destroying inbound asteroids. One is to hit it and destroy it with a nuclear weapon, but if it didn't annihilate it completely, that would turn a cannon ball into a cluster bomb. Rocks would rain down and destroy anyway. Better to detonate an atomic bomb nearby and try to deflect the asteroid.

Other ideas are to use lasers to cause the rock's gases to burn off and gently steer it off course or to use mirrors to concentrate the heat of the sun to cause the gases to ignite.[32]

Whatever they try, it may break the asteroid apart, but the devastation caused by falling rocks will still destroy Babylon and the cities of the nations. Many countries will be desolate. Egypt will be so hard hit that no one will live there for the next 40 years. The Lord said,

> I will bring a **sword** upon thee, and cut off man and beast out of thee. And the land of Egypt shall be desolate and waste . . . I am against thee, and against thy rivers, and I will make the land of Egypt utterly **waste and desolate, from the tower of Syene even unto the border of Ethio-**

pia. No foot of man shall pass through it, nor foot of beast shall pass through it, neither shall it be inhabited forty years.[33]

The Noise of His Tabernacle

Job 36:29 asks, "Also can any understand the spreadings of the clouds, or **the noise of his tabernacle.**" We can now understand how noise can be associated with the tabernacle. When the asteroid strikes, the noise will be heard around the world.

A noise shall come even to the ends of the earth; for the LORD hath a controversy with the nations, he will plead with all flesh; he will give them that are wicked to the sword, saith the LORD.[34]

A Free Gift

Please see to it that you take advantage of our wonderful Saviour's offer to save you. Don't put it off until it is too late. It is his free gift to you, but you have to accept it.

For by grace are ye saved through faith; and that not of yourselves: **it is the gift of God:** Not of works, lest any man should boast. For we are his workmanship, created in Christ Jesus unto good works, which God hath before ordained that we should walk in them.[35]

Pray. Say that you accept the Lord Jesus Christ as your own personal Saviour. Your prayer of faith is evidence that you accept God's gift. Tell someone about it. Make it a done deed.

> The word is nigh thee, even in thy mouth, and in thy heart: that is, the word of faith, which we preach; That if thou shalt confess with thy mouth the Lord Jesus, and shalt believe in thine heart that God hath raised him from the dead, thou shalt be saved. For with the heart man believeth unto righteousness; and with the mouth confession is made unto salvation.[36]

We have found that there is a payback, but it is up to the Lord to execute it. He said, "Vengeance is mine. I will repay."

His "device" is against Babylon. He will toss the asteroid "like a ball into a large country."

The "destroying mountain" will come from between the planets and clash with Earth seven months before the Lord returns. The worst damage will run from the Euphrates River to the Nile.

This impact explosion is "the vengeance of his temple." It will be the worst thing to happen to Earth since Adam was put on it.

Be sure to take advantage of the chance set before you to get off this planet before "the curse" strikes such fear into men that they will hold their sides as if feeling birth pangs. Hearts will fail from fear. You don't want to be here then.

Instead, participate in the Marriage of the Lamb in heaven that day. It will take place after Jesus is called to the assembly and receives his crown. After the wedding, he will again drink wine with his disciples. The marriage in Cana, where Jesus turned water into wine was a type.

> AND the third day (in the third millennium) there was a marriage in Cana (''the nest'') of Galilee (''the revolution of the wheel,'' i.e., on the Lord's planet that orbits like a wheel); and the mother of Jesus was there: And both Jesus was called, and his disciples, to the marriage.[37]

4 ✢ The Secret of His Tabernacle

I'M AWESTRUCK JUST THINKING WHAT A PRIVI-
lege it is to find this out. It makes me want to whisper.
As if the mysteries of the chariot of the cherubim and
the vengeance of his temple weren't enough, the tabernacle contains another secret, one that we never dared
hope to have revealed to us ahead of time—the location
of heaven.

Listen as a Tribulation saint speaks of "the time
of Jacob's trouble,"[1] Rapture II, and the secret of the
Lord's tabernacle:

> For in the time of trouble he shall hide me in his
> pavilion: **in the secret of his tabernacle shall he
> hide me; he shall set me up upon a rock.**[2]

In Hebrew, the word translated "pavilion" is *cok*,
pavilion, tabernacle, tent, or house. He will hide the
Tribulation saints in his heavenly home. The Lord's

dwelling place, palace and throne are on this heavenly rock, just as the temple area in Jerusalem is located on a rock.

The phrase about hiding them in his pavilion is parallel to the one about hiding them in the secret of his tabernacle. It is the same thing restated in different terms. Therefore, if his pavilion is heaven, the secret of his tabernacle also refers to heaven, and they are both "up" upon a celestial rock.

Starting with the information given in Psalms 27:4 and tying it in with a few related things we have gleaned from Scripture, we can figure out quite a lot about Rapture II:

1. It will take place in the time of trouble.
   a. The time of Jacob's trouble is day 2,300 of the shortened Tribulation.[3]
   b. It is the first day of the millennial Day of the Lord.[4]
   c. It will fall on the Feast of Trumpets[5] right after this age ends on the Day of Preparation.[6]
2. The Lord will hide them in his own heavenly pavilion.
3. He will hide them in the secret of his tabernacle.
4. He will set them up upon another rock.
5. Their new dwelling place is in the heavenly city.

The Secret Place of The Most High

Both the Church saints, who go to heaven in Rapture I before the Tribulation, and the Tribulation saints, who

go in Rapture II on the last day of the 2,300-day shortened Tribulation, will dwell in the secret place of the
most High. This is the secret place of our Lord Jesus
Christ, who is the Almighty.[7]

> HE that dwelleth in **the secret place of the most
> High** shall abide under the shadow of the Al-
> mighty. . . . He shall cover thee with his feathers,
> and under his wings shalt thou trust . . . Thou
> shalt not be afraid for the terror by night; nor for
> the arrow that flieth by day . . . nor for the de-
> struction that wasteth at noonday . . . Only with
> thine eyes shalt thou behold and see the reward
> of the wicked. Because thou hast made the
> LORD, which is my refuge, even the most High,
> thy habitation.[8]

The "terror by night" will be caused by the knowledge of what is heading our way. Even men will put
their hands on their abdomen as if in birth pain. The
"arrow that flieth by day" is the same as the flaming
sword, which is the asteroid. It explodes in flames as
it hits our atmosphere and will strike at noon, causing
"the destruction that wasteth at noonday."

The saints who are taken to heaven in Rapture I will
be kept from the Tribulation. This is evident in Revelation 3:10 as well as Psalms 31:19–21 which follows.
They will dwell in the Lord's presence in his pavilion
in a strong city, which is New Jerusalem.

> Oh how great is thy goodness . . . which thou
> hast wrought for them that trust in thee before
> the sons of men! Thou shalt hide them in the
> secret of thy presence **from** the pride of man (the

False Prophet): thou shalt keep them secretly in a pavilion **from** the strife (*riyb,* multitude) of tongues (the many languages spoken by the united nations). Blessed be the LORD: for he hath shewed me his marvellous kindness in a strong city.

The multitude of tongues at the Tower of Babel was a type of the final Babylon, the headquarters of the world church and world government. After their one language became many, they stopped building the city and scattered across the face of the Earth. Immediately after this age ends, they will stop building Babylon. It will be no more.

The Planet Called Heaven

Heaven is not a shoulder shrugging who knows where? It is another orbiting stone out there in his heavenly tent, similar to Earth. In the Septuagint, Job 38:37,38 asks,

(Who) is he that numbers the clouds in wisdom, and has **bowed the heaven** . . . to the earth (i.e., as viewed from Earth)? For it (heaven) is spread out **as dusty earth,** and I have cemented it as one hewn stone to another (i.e., formed it by coalescence).

Since Earth is a planet, and heaven is "spread out as dusty earth," heaven is also a planet. The astronomers have wondered whether this particular planet has a rocky core or not. The Bible shows that it does. They have also thought that the planets were formed from the coalescence of planetesimals. Scripture supports this hypothesis.

The Sapphire: A Symbol

When Moses saw God on Mount Sinai, which represented heaven,

> there was under his feet as it were a paved work of **a sapphire stone,** and as it were the **body of heaven** (heavenly body) in *his* clearness (*tohar,* glory).[9]

The sapphire stone symbolized the Lord's throne on a heavenly body and furnished us an excellent clue to its location.

When Ezekiel saw his second vision of the four cherubim, which are our terrestrial planets, he saw a sapphire stone in an orbit farther out from the sun than the cherubims. He said,

> (In) the firmament (vault of space) that was **above the head of the cherubims** there appeared over them **as it were** (symbolic language) **a sapphire stone, as the appearance of the likeness of a throne.**[10]

The sapphire stone is a symbol that represents another planet. The throne of the God of Israel is on it. Ezekiel also said that the cherubim lifted up their wings

> and mounted up from the earth in my sight . . . and the glory of the God of Israel was over them above. This is the living creature (lively thing) that I saw **under the God of Israel** by the river

of Chebar; and I knew that they (the four plus the one under the God of Israel) were the cherubims.[11]

Lifting up their wings is figurative language indicating flight. The four terrestrial planets are flying their orbits, and the God of Israel is on another planet orbiting farther out in space. Therefore, his glory is "over them above." Not only are the terrestrial planets called cherubim here, the planet under the God of Israel is also referred to as a cherubim.

The Lord's throne is on one of the ten heavenly bodies in his heavenly tent. It is farther out in space than the terrestrial planets, so it is beyond Mars. He sits between the cherubim, so it isn't on Mercury or Pluto, the outside planets. Therefore, it is probably on one of the giant planets that has a rocky core. Only four choices are left, Jupiter, Saturn, Uranus and Neptune. All four are giant planets.

HEAVEN: A GIANT PLANET

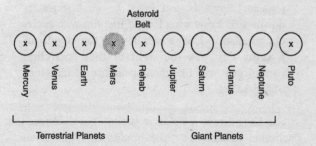

Heaven is not on the terrestrial planet,
oron Rahab, which split apart,
or on the outside ones

In Ezekiel 1:22,26–28 in the New English Bible, the sapphire throne is mentioned with another important clue added. There is a ring of radiance around the throne like the appearance of the glory of the LORD. It glitters in the sunlight like ice.

> Above the heads of the living creatures (cherubim) was, as it were, a vault **glittering like a sheet of ice** . . . Above the vault over their heads there appeared, as it were, **a sapphire in the shape of a throne,** and high above all, upon the throne, a form in human likeness.

This glittering sheet of ice ties in with Revelation 4:6 (NEB), where **"a sea of glass, like a sheet of ice,"** is stretched out in front of the Lord's throne. Revelation 15:2 calls it "a sea of glass shot with fire."

Continuing, Ezekiel said,

> I saw what might have been brass (golden clouds) glowing like fire in a furnace from the waist (equator) upwards; and from the waist (equator) downwards I saw what looked like fire with encircling radiance. **Like a rainbow in the clouds on a rainy day was the sight of that encircling radiance;** it was like the appearance of the glory of the LORD.

The King James Version is similar, but describes the encircling radiance as "the brightness round about." We do have one unique planet in our solar system that stands out from all the rest because of its golden clouds surrounded by a spectacular halo of ice rings around the equator.

There is more to learn about this beautiful rainbow with its myriads of ice crystals reflecting color like a sea of prisms in the unfiltered sunlight. We will come back to it later.

A GOLDEN GLOBE WITH ICY RINGS

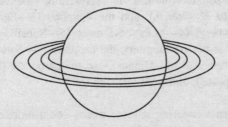

Edom means red, Satan's color, and in Obadiah 1:3,4, the Lord went beyond Edom and addressed Satan. Evidently, Satan was king of the planet Rahab in the past and is still king of an asteroid called Wormwood, a broken chunk of the former planet Rahab.

> The pride of thine heart hath deceived thee, thou that dwellest in the clefts (*chavag,* places of refuge) of the rock, whose habitation is high; that saith in his heart, Who shall bring me down to the ground? Though thou exalt thyself as the eagle, and though thou set **thy nest among the stars,** thence will I bring thee down, saith the LORD.

Similarly, in Ezekiel 28:12–18, God spoke to Satan as king of Tyrus. The word Tyrus means rock, so he was actually addressing Satan as king of the rock. He said,

> Thou hast been in Eden the garden of God (both the earthly and heavenly Paradise); every precious stone (planet) was thy covering (surroundings), the sardius (number 1, representing Mercury), topaz (2—Venus), and the diamond (3—Earth), the beryl (4—Mars), the onyx (5—Rahab), and the jasper (6—Jupiter), the sapphire (7—Saturn), the emerald (8—Uranus), and the carbuncle (9—Neptune), and gold (10—Pluto).

When wondering if these stones could represent the planets, I casually looked up sapphire in my desk dictionary[12] and got an electrifying shock.

The word sapphire is from the Hebrew *sappir,* which is from the Sanskrit *sanipriya,* literally, **dear to the planet Saturn,** from *Sani,* **Saturn,** plus *priya,* **dear.**

Remember when the Israelites were at Sinai, God referred to the mountain of Sinai as "the body of heaven"? Sinai, of which the derivation seems to be unknown, must come from the Sanskrit *Sani,* Saturn. God appeared on a pavement of sapphire to help us make the connection.[13]

The Hebrew form, *sappir,* or *cappayr,* is from the Hebrew root *caphar,* to shew forth, speak, talk, tell, declare, number. It does seem as if the sapphire symbol is trying to tell us something. The name has a concrete connection with Saturn, and if it is the Lord's throne, it is certainly dear—it's Paradise. It is appropriately listed in the seventh place, for seven is God's number.

Seven means completion and perfection. The writer of Hebrews said that heaven was a better country or fatherland,[14] so seven fits it well. A lot of sevens in Revelation have a connection with heaven, seven stars in Jesus' hand, seven candlesticks, seven horns, seven eyes, seven Spirits of God, seven seals on the Book of the Purchase of Earth, seven trumpets, seven thunders and seven vials.

In The Midst of The Stones of Fire

Ezekiel shows that Satan's planet was in the middle of the planetary lineup. The Lord said to Satan,

> Thou art the anointed cherub that covereth (*cakak,* guards): and I have set thee so: thou wast upon the holy mountain of God;[15] thou hast walked up and down in the midst of the stones of fire (on the fifth planet). . . . thou hast sinned: therefore I will cast thee as profane out of the mountain of God (number 7—Saturn): and I will destroy thee, O covering (*cakak,* guarding) cherub, **from the midst of the stones of fire** (from number 5—Rahab). . . . (and) I will bring thee **to ashes upon the earth** (by the asteroid impact).[16]

Here two pictures are blended into one. Satan is the anointed cherub that guards the way to the tree of life,[17] and his planet is the cherubim that guards the way. The word translated anointed is *mimshach,* outspread or expansion. The Vulgate has *Cherub extentus,* as if the cherubim extended wings. Actually, Satan's planet blew up. It expanded in a big burst of fireworks, and its pieces formed the Asteroid Belt.

A Precious Stone in The Foil of a Ring

When the bride described her beloved (i.e., Jesus Christ) in the Song of Solomon 4:10–16, we find a lot of symbolism. White ruddy skin and black hair seem literal since Jesus was Jewish, and that language is very definite—"My beloved is . . . His head is." Yet when you get to verse 14, it is hard to imagine how "His hands are as gold rings set with the beryl."

A lot in this passage is symbolic and seems to go beyond his person to give us hints as to where he is located. Examine passages carefully when you see "like" or "as." They denote symbolic language. Look for double meanings too. Here, it speaks of eyes then goes beyond that and seems to be talking about orbs or spheres.

> My beloved is white and ruddy, the chiefest among ten thousand. His head is as the most fine gold, his locks are bushy, and black as a raven.

This far, the only symbolic part is the head "as the most fine gold." Because of the word "as," we know for sure that we are to take it symbolically. Gold represents deity and is very fitting here. As the description goes on, it gets more symbolic.

> His eyes are as the eyes of doves by the rivers of waters,

The dove is the symbol of the Holy Spirit. Since Jesus Christ is God, this certainly applies to him personally. The rivers of waters probably refer to the "pure river of water of life . . . proceeding out of the throne of God and of the Lamb" in heaven.[18] The next part begins to sound more like it is describing where he lives. Continuing, the Song of Solomon says of the eyes

washed with milk (the orbs look opaque and whitish as we look up at them with our naked eyes in the night sky), and fitly set (margin: 'set as a precious stone in the foil of a ring,' i.e., the 'sapphire' planet and her rings). . . . His hands (*yad*, borders) are as gold rings set with the beryl: his belly is as bright ivory (i.e., the light golden clouds) overlaid with sapphires (a symbol of Saturn).

Beryl is the color of the wheels, or orbits, in Ezekiel 1:16 and 10:9. The deep-green variety of beryl is the emerald, which stood for Judah, the tribe of Jesus Christ, in the breastplate of the high priest. This emerald color showing in the rings agrees with Revelation 4:3: "and there was a rainbow round about the throne, in sight like unto an emerald." A greenish outer edge does show up sometimes in photographs taken with earth-bound telescopes, as it does in one I have.

The Asteroid Threat

The broken piece of the planet Rahab threatens us about twice a year as it crosses our orbit. It will end up as ashes upon the Earth at the end of this age. In 2007, it is due to strike at noon as the millennial Day of the Lord begins on the Jewish New Year Day, which is the Feast of Trumpets. Scripture says,

And it shall come to pass in that day, saith the Lord GOD, that I will cause the sun to go down

at noon, and I will darken the earth in the clear day; And I will turn your **feasts** into mourning.[19]

When he (the Satan-possessed False Prophet) is about to fill his belly, God shall cast the fury of his wrath upon him, and shall rain it upon him **while he is eating. . . . the glittering sword** (the flaming sword of Genesis 3:24) cometh out of his gall: terrors are upon him. . . . . The increase of his house shall depart . . . This is the portion of a wicked man from God.[20]

The most wicked man of all time is the Satan-possessed False Prophet.

Babylon fell at the time of a feast the day of the handwriting on the wall. That was a type of the final destruction of Babylon on a feast day.

The Day of God's Wrath is on one of the seven feasts the Lord gave to Israel. When you find out when end-time events are scheduled to take place, you will be able to see that God first figured out when certain important things were going to happen and then set the seven feasts on those days.

In the following table, remember that in a Jewish day, which starts at 6:00 P.M., there are first 12 hours of night then 12 hours of daylight that have to be accounted for. If we think in terms of our days, it is easy to skip an entire day.

THE SEVEN FEASTS AND POSSIBLE FULFILLMENTS

Preparation Day for Passover

Thu. 13 Nisan 4-6-30 A.D.

Last Supper, soon after Thursday began (our Wed. eve.)

The Sanhedrin met on their regular meeting day,
    Thursday They convened early, during the night
    portion

Crucifixion, 9:00 A.M.

Death of Christ, about 3:00 P.M.

Passover Lambs killed between 3:00 and 5:00 P.M.

1. Passover   Fri. 14 Nisan 4-7-30 A.D.
    High sabbath
    Burial of Christ
    Preparation Day for Saturday Sabbath
    Passover lambs eaten

2. Unleavened Bread, Sabbath
                     Sat. 15 Nisan 4-8-30 A.D.

3. Firstfruits   Sun. 16 Nisan 4-9-30 A.D.
    Resurrection of Christ

4. Pentecost (the Feast of Weeks)
    Birth of church on Earth
                     Sun. 6 Sivan 5-28-30 A.D.
    Birth of church to Heaven
                     Sun. 6 Sivan   5-31-1998
    Beg. of 70th Week of Daniel
                     M. 6 Sivan   5-28-2001

5. Trumpets   Thu: 1 Tishri   9-13-2007
    "that day" (Old Testament term)
    Beginning of Millennium
    Christ crowned on his birthday in heaven
    Marriage of the Lamb in heaven
    Rapture of Tribulation Saints to heaven
    Judgment—Believers rewarded in heaven
    Judgment—Nonbelievers reap the whirlwind on
    Earth
    Sign of the Son of Man seen on Earth
    Marriage Supper of the Lamb in heaven

Days of Awe, between Trumpets and Atonement

Israel's remnant has seen the Sign, the Lord has saved their country; therefore they realize that the New Testament is true, and Jesus Christ is their Messiah

6. Atonement   Sat. 10 Tishri   9-22-2007
Israel's remnant seeks forgiveness on the Sabbath Day

7. Tabernacles   Thu. 15 Tishri   9-27-2007
Ingathering of Israel; Scriptures Read to them; Rejoicing

For information on how to figure out when these things will take place, see *Exit: 2007, The Secret of Secrets Revealed.*

The Day of Atonement falls on the Saturday sabbath in 2007. This is perfect. The Lord's instructions included

It shall be unto you a sabbath of rest, and ye shall afflict your souls: in the ninth day of the month at even, from even unto even, shall ye celebrate your sabbath (Leviticus 23:32).

One of the feasts, the Feast of Trumpets, will be the great day of destruction. Scripture says,

O ye priests . . . If ye will not hear, and if ye will not lay it to heart, to give glory unto my name, saith the LORD of hosts, I will even send **a curse** upon you . . . **your solemn feasts; and one shall take you away with it.**[21]

What will ye do in the solemn day, and in the day of **the feast of the LORD?** For, lo, they are gone because of **destruction** . . . The days of visitation are come, the days of recompense are come; Israel shall know it: the prophet (the False Prophet of Israel) is a fool (he's Satan-possessed), the spiritual man (the Beast of Rome) is mad (he's Satan-obsessed).[22]

From the many scriptures that speak of blowing the trumpets, we know it is the Feast of Trumpets.

BLOW ye the **trumpet** in Zion, and sound an alarm . . . for the day of the LORD (the first day of the Millennium) cometh . . . A day of darkness . . . there hath not been ever the like, neither shall be any more after it.[23]

That day is a day of wrath, a day of trouble and distress . . . a day of clouds and thick darkness, **A day of the trumpet and alarm.**[24]

Do you know that our astronomers have found 310 NEAs, Near Earth Asteroids, and find new ones all the time? They have even found an unsettling number, at least 50, between us and our moon. The flaming sword (*chereb,* a hunk of a former cherubim) is out there threatening us all right.

The astronomers now realize that when we have been able to view the surface of other heavenly bodies, they have all been cratered. This is why the symbolic cherubim in the tabernacle were made of beaten gold. Even our moon is pockmarked, and Earth is not immune. We have at least 100 identified craters on this planet.

In 1991, at San Juan Capistrano, CA, during a meeting with prominent astronomers from around the world, we were told that they definitely expect an asteroid to crash into Earth sometime, maybe within the next 30 years. About a dozen experts from around the world were already working on a missile system to try to deflect an incoming asteroid. Half of them were present at that meeting and stood to be recognized.

I heard after that that scientists had asked NASA to place a hydrogen bomb station in space that could blow an asteroid up before it could collide with Earth. However, Scripture shows that their efforts will be in vain, and it only takes a rock 0.7 of a mile in diameter to wipe out civilization.

Eleanor Helin is a planetary scientist from Jet Propulsion Laboratory who searches for asteroids at Mount Palomar Observatory. She told me at that meeting in San Juan Capistrano that she would run orbits on the computer and try to figure out what asteroid might be in a position to hit us on September 13, 2007.

She keeps looking and finding more and more asteroids. So do others. The total number of known NEAs she announced in San Juan Capistrano was 144, now it is up to 310. Just recently, she said, **"Earth is embedded in a swarm of asteroids"** and **"We don't get hit often. But when we do, it can be catastrophic. We need to look for what's out there and what's headed our way."**[25]

In the Orange County Register, July 22, 1994, an article was headlined, "Lawmaker aims for Earth to avoid the fate of Jupiter." Representative Ralph Hall (a Democrat from Texas), chairman of the House space subcommittee said, "If a comet or asteroid the size of the one we have been watching hit Jupiter this week were to hit the Earth, it would cause a major global catastrophe." He says, "If a head-on collision is coming, there is a remedy: Hit the intruder with a nuclear missile. Or, given time, send up a spacecraft to nudge it off course.''

I hate to tell him that they can try, but it won't work. They might knock it apart, but rocks will still fall and do their dirty work. You can trust the Bible. God's prophecies come true 100%. If the Bible says it, it will happen right on schedule in spite of everything anyone can do. Revelation 16:21 says,

> And there fell upon men a great hail out of heaven, every stone about the weight of a talent (about 100 pounds): and men blasphemed God because of the plague of the hail; for the plague thereof was exceeding great.

''Astronomers tell us,'' Hall said, ''that **each day, an asteroid the size of a house passes within the distance between the Earth and the moon. . . . Each month, one the size of a football field passes within that distance.''**

That is scary, and our chances of not getting a warning are great. On March 23, 1989, a 1,000-foot-diameter asteroid only missed Earth by six hours, and the astronomers didn't know it until it had already passed us. That is too close for comfort. If it comes straight at us, it may not be recognized.

Last year NASA sampled the higher altitudes and determined that a large celestial object had plunged into the Pacific Ocean. This emphasizes two things, that the astronomers do not always know ahead of time that we are going to get hit and that the Earth is not immune to collision.

When the pieces of comet Shoemaker-Levy 9 (which

could have been an asteroid instead of a comet) hit Jupiter in July, 1994, it showed what can happen. The force released was probably greater than all the atomic bombs ever made. Some impacts had a force of over 20 million megatons. Fireballs rose up to 1,800 miles above the visible surface of Jupiter. A white cloud more than 10,000 miles across was visible in Jupiter's atmosphere when fragment G hit.

It is interesting to note that the first piece of comet Shoemaker-Levy 9 hit Jupiter on Tisha Be'Av (Av 9 on the Jewish Calendar, our Saturday evening, July, 16, 1994). This is the Jewish fast commemorating the last day that both temples, Solomon's and Herod's, still stood. Both were burned on the same date, Av 10.[26] Is this rain of at least 21 rocks on Jupiter a sign to help us understand the prophecies?[27]

Ground Zero

The flaming sword will strike at Babylon. This will be the third time the Sword of the Lord has struck Earth. The Lord said to Ezekiel,

> Son of man, prophesy, and say, Thus saith the LORD; Say, A sword, a sword is sharpened, and also furbished: It is sharpened to make a sore slaughter, it is furbished that it may glitter . . . **let the sword be doubled the third time.**[28]

The first time must have been when the dinosaurs died. The second was when Sodom and Gomorrah and the cities of the plains were destroyed. The third is when Babylon will be destroyed, which will be twice as big a catastrophe as when Sodom and Gomorrah were destroyed, and that one split the Earth and formed the Great Rift Valley.

That crack extends from Turkey down the Jordan Valley and on down to Lake Nyasa in Africa. The bedrock below the Dead Sea was punched down 2,615 feet below sea level. The earth still shivers there at times.

According to Ezekiel 21:16,18 in the Confraternity Version, God gave this sword "over to the burnisher" (Lucifer, light bearer, i.e., Satan) and "the sword has been tested." An asteroid has hit Earth before and caused great devastation.

Josephus, the Jewish historian that lived in Jesus' day, reported that in his time,

> "Traces of the five cities are still to be seen, as well as the ashes growing in their fruits, which fruits have a colour as if they were fit to be eaten but if you pluck them with your hand, they dissolve into smoke and ashes."[29]

A large cemetery has been found at the ruins of Babedh-Dhra, thought to be Sodom, southeast of the Dead Sea. A lot of people lived in that area. Nearby Numeira is thought to be Gomorrah. At three sites that have been excavated near the Dead Sea, archaeologists found that all three were terminated abruptly. Beneath the rubble, clear evidence of the fiery conflagration that destroyed the cities of the plain has been found. An ash layer blankets the top of the city ruins.[30]

Flaming Sword Deposes The False Prophet

On the day the flaming sword hits Earth, the False Prophet will be deposed as head of the world church and of the world government. He will lose both the mitre and the crown. The Lord said,

> I have set the point of the sword against all their gates . . . it is made bright (ignites when it hits our atmosphere), it is wrapped up for the slaughter. . . . And thou, profane wicked prince of Israel, whose day is come, when iniquity shall have an end . . . **Remove the diadem** (*mitsnepheth*, **mitre;** i.e., he's head of the world church[31]), **and take off the crown** (he's also head of the world government[32]): . . . I will overturn, overturn, overturn, it: and it shall be no more, until he come whose right it is (Christ, whose return is seven months later[33]); and I will give it him.[34]

The Beast of Revelation 13:1–10 is head of the world church at the beginning of the Tribulation.[35] He is also elected head of the world government[36] and will rule 42 months,[37] the first half of the Tribulation. After 42 months, I believe he will have an accident and the False Prophet of Revelation 13:11–18 will take over both offices.

> And he exerciseth all the power of the first beast before him, and causeth the earth and them which dwell therein to worship the first beast, whose deadly wound was healed.

Although the Satan-possessed False Prophet rules, the first beast is still around when Christ returns. At the end of the battle of Armageddon, both are mentioned.

> And the beast was taken, and with him the false prophet that wrought miracles before him, with

which he deceived them that had received the mark of the beast, and them that worshipped his image. These both were cast alive into a lake of fire burning with brimstone.

This lake of fire burning with brimstone will be formed by the asteroid impact. It will cover 1,600 furlongs, or 181.8 miles.[38]

For it is the day of the LORD'S vengeance, and the year of recompenses for the controversy of Zion. And the streams thereof shall be turned into pitch, and the dust thereof into brimstone, and the land thereof shall become burning pitch. It shall not be quenched night nor day; the smoke thereof shall go up for ever.[39]

I wonder if they will have to say, "Good-bye" to the petroleum industry of that oil rich land. Those tremendous reserves are an accident waiting to happen. Isaiah 9:5 says that "this shall be with burning and fuel of fire." Jeremiah 51:58 in the NIV shows that at Babylon, "the nations' labor is only fuel for the flames."

The asteroid is called the curse in Zechariah 5:3,4. It will hit the house of the Roman Beast and the house of the Israeli False Prophet after the headquarters of the world church and world government are moved to Babylon in "the land of Shinar."[40] The Lord said that he would bring forth the curse himself.

This is the curse that goeth forth over the face of the whole earth: for every one that stealeth shall be cut off as on this side according to it; and every one that sweareth shall be cut off as on that side according to it. **I will bring it forth, saith the LORD of hosts,** and it shall enter into the house of the thief (the False Prophet), and into the house of him (the Beast) that sweareth falsely by my name: and it shall remain in the midst of his house, and shall consume it with the timber thereof and the stones thereof.

The Rainbow Surrounding The Throne

In Revelation 4, John was taken to heaven. The first thing he saw there was a throne. It sounds like it could be on Saturn.

He that sat on the throne was "like a jasper and a sardine stone." These are the first and last stones in the breastplate worn by the high priest. This signifies that Jesus is our great high priest.

It also shows that he is the first and the last as he told us in Revelation 1:17 and 22:13. This means that he is both Yahweh of the Old Testament and Y'shua (Iesous in Greek), Jesus, of the new. As Yahweh, he was the pre-incarnate Christ. As Y'shua, he is the incarnate Christ.

In Revelation 4:2 and 5:6, he is both the one sitting "on the throne" and the Lamb "in the midst of the throne."

Revelation 4:3–6 continues,

there was a rainbow round about the throne, in sight like unto an emerald. . . . and **there were seven lamps of fire burning before the throne,** which are the seven Spirits of God. And before the throne **there was a sea of glass like unto crystal.**

The emerald was the stone in the breastplate that stood for Judah, the tribe of Jesus. This shows that this is Jesus Christ sitting on the throne.

The rainbow around the throne and the sea of glass like crystal (or **ice,** as in the NEB) sound like the rings around Saturn, but what are the seven lamps of fire (flaming torches in the NEB) burning before the throne? Here they are called Spirits of God.

Since they are lamps or torches, and before the throne instead of in the midst of it, they may not be the same as the Spirits of God of Revelation 5:6.

In Revelation 5:6, the Lamb (Christ) is "in the midst of the throne" and has "seven horns (representing his omnipotence) and seven eyes (his omniscience), which are the seven Spirits of God (his omnipresence) sent forth into all the earth." These stand for the complete perfect Spirit of God residing in Christ and sent to Earth. "For it pleased the Father that in him should all fulness dwell."[41] Jesus Christ demonstrated the character of his Father to us. He "is the image (*eikon,* likeness) of the invisible God."[42]

However, if the lamps before the throne stand for something else, what do they represent? Could these spirits represent the same things as the flying creatures that looked like lamps that Ezekiel saw in his visions?

Ezekiel 1:21 says that "the **spirit** of the living creature was in the wheels." The word translated spirit is *ruwach,* and means wind, breath, current of air or region of the sky. There was a propelling current of air or wind in these orbits in the sky.

Ezekiel's visions are filled with symbolism. The four cherubim are characterized as living creatures with four wings, yet in Ezekiel 1:13, "their appearance was **like burning coals of fire, and like the appearance of lamps**" orbiting in the sky.

They were not actually alive, but lively *planetes,* wanderers in Latin (Greek *planasthai,* to wander). They did not have wings, but flew. They were not lamps, but were lit up like lamps. They did not have eyes, but were themselves spheres or full orbs, just as the Latin *orbis terrarum* applies to the globe of the Earth. They did not have high rings full of eyes, as the translators thought, but high orbits. They did not have actual wheels within wheels, but concentric orbits. They were not burning coals, but planets reflecting the sunlight. They did not have four faces, but faced all four directions.

The same faces were on the banners placed at the compass points on the sides of the Israelite camp in the wilderness. Dan's flag with an eagle on it was placed on the north. Ephraim's with the ox on it was placed on the west. Reuben's with a man pictured on it was stationed on the south side. Since Jesus is of the tribe of Judah and is to return as a lion, it is significant that Judah's flag with the lion on it was stationed on the **east side.** Christ's heavenly throne is mapped out as being east of Eden. The celestial map of our solar system starts with the sun on the west and ends with Pluto on the east.

Ezekiel saw what looked like lamps or coals of fire orbiting the sun, and John saw what looked like seven lamps or flaming torches. Do they both stand for heavenly bodies? Are these lamps of fire **before the throne** the Sun, Mercury, Venus, Earth, Mars, Rahab and Jupiter?

SEVEN LAMPS OF FIRE BEFORE THE THRONE

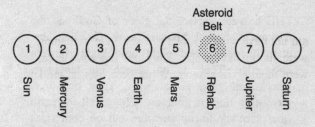

Sun | Mercury | Venus | Earth | Mars | Rahab | Jupiter | Saturn

Seraphim

Revelation 4:6 describes four beasts that sound like cherubim, except the cherubim have four wings. It says,

> (In) the midst of the throne, and round about the throne, were four beasts full of eyes (full orbs) before and behind (i.e., they are spheres) . . . And the four beasts had each of them six wings about him; and they were full of eyes (full orbs, spheres) within: and they rest not day and night, saving Holy, holy, holy, Lord God Almighty.

These are identical to the seraphims Isaiah saw. In chapter 6, verses 1–3, Isaiah

> saw also the Lord sitting upon a throne, high and lifted up, and his train (hem, robe of light) filled the temple. Above it stood the seraphims (which means burners): each one had six wings . . . And

one cried unto another, and said, Holy, holy, holy,
is the LORD of hosts.

They do not have to be alive to utter this kind of speech
for Psalms 19:1 says,

THE heavens declare the glory of God; and the
firmament sheweth his handiwork. Day unto day
uttereth speech, and night unto night sheweth
knowledge. There is no speech nor language,
where their voice is not heard. Their line (*qav,*
measuring line) is gone out through all the earth
(the planetary lineup stretches out on both sides
of the Earth), and their words to the end of the
world.

In the King James Version quoted above, the four
seraphim are described as in the midst and round about
the throne. They could be the planets Jupiter, Uranus,
Neptune, and Pluto, that orbit near Saturn. The word
translated "midst" is *meso,* which means among, between or before them. That provides us another clue.
Since Jupiter's orbit is closer to us, it is **before them,**
before Saturn and the other outer planets. The orbits of
the other three planets are outside Saturn's orbit, so
they orbit **around** Saturn. Similar to the Amplified
Bible and Vincent's translation, the Berkeley Version
says that

Around the throne, **in the center of each side,**
there were four living beings full of eyes in front
and behind; the first living being like a lion, the
second like a bullock, the third with a manlike
face and the fourth like a flying eagle.

That the heavenly bodies were symbolically positioned in the center of each side around the throne makes sense because the four flags placed at the compass points around the tabernacle had on them the faces of a lion, a bullock, a man and an eagle. These faces represent the four directions.

On the tabernacle curtains, all ten original planets were depicted as cherubim. However, after we learn that Satan's planet Rahab was split apart and became the asteroid belt, another picture emerges. Omitting Rahab from the five terrestrial planets leaves the four present cherubim, Mercury, Venus, Earth and Mars. These were what Ezekiel saw in his visions of the heavens.

It seems that the throne of the Lord is among the outer planets. Saturn is the second largest one. Around it are four heavenly bodies. With respect to distance from the sun, Jupiter precedes Saturn, and Uranus, Neptune, and Pluto follow it. Do you think that the four six-winged seraphim around the throne of the Lord could represent Jupiter, Uranus, Neptune, and Pluto?

Evidently, all the planets can be designated as cherubim, as the cherubim embroidered on the tabernacle curtains. Or, taking into consideration that Rahab split and the asteroid belt now separates the inner from the outer planets, the inner ones can be called cherubim and the outer ones surrounding the throne can be called seraphim. Since the word seraphim means burners, they also have the appearance of lamps.

The cherubim may have been characterized with four wings because they are the first four planets. The seraphim may have been given six wings because Jupiter, the first seraphim, was originally the sixth planet in our solar system.

CHERUBIM AND SERAPHIM

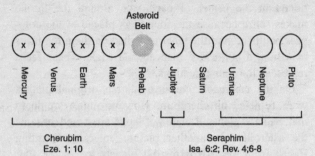

It seems that all of the ten planets can be called cherubim, as on the ten curtains, but only the outer planets surrounding the Lord's throne can also be called seraphim.

Enthroned on a Cherubim

John saw the Lamb "inside the **circle** of living creatures" (Revelation 5:6, NEB). Thus, the four planets are around the throne as Jupiter, Uranus, Neptune, and Pluto are as they orbit around.

When the Lord is crowned and begins his reign, he will marry his bride and then begin to judge. Psalms 99:1 says, "let the people tremble, **he sitteth** *between* **the cherubims;** let the earth be moved (it will totter when the asteroid hits). This is when all planets are called cherubims.

If the King James is translated correctly, and "he sitteth between the cherubims," his throne could be between Jupiter and Uranus. However, Green's Interlinear says, "**(He) sits (on) the cherubim**," and the Jerusalem Bible has "**he is enthroned on the winged creatures.**" First Samuel 4:4 (RSV) speaks of "the LORD of hosts, who is **enthroned on the cherubim.**"

First Chronicles 13:6 (Green) says, "God Jehovah, who **dwells among the cherubs.**"

It seems that the Lord is enthroned on one of the ten cherubim, but between two other cherubim, therefore not on the first or the last. This quickly eliminates the two smallest planets, Mercury and Pluto. We have already eliminated the terrestrial planets anyway, so the only possibilities left are the giant planets, Jupiter, Saturn, Uranus, and Neptune as determined before.

The Clouds Shining Like Gold

The clues have all pointed to Saturn as being the throne of God and the Lamb. Saturn is shrouded in golden clouds. We have never seen its surface. Even this ties in.

> O LORD . . . Who coverest thyself with light as with a garment: who stretchest out the heavens like a curtain (the ten curtains of the tabernacle): Who layeth the beams of his chambers (upper rooms[43]) in the waters: **who maketh the clouds his chariot:** who walketh upon the wings (quarters, i.e., orbits) of the wind.[44]

As we saw before, Job 36:32;37:18–22 in the Septuagint shows that heaven has to be visible to some from Earth:

> He has hidden the light in his hands, and given charge concerning it to the interposing cloud. . . . the foundations for the ancient **heavens?** they are strong as a molten (cast) mirror . . . But **the light is not visible to all: it shines afar off in the heavens** . . . From the north come the **clouds**

**shining like gold: in these great are the glory
and honour of the Almighty** (because it is his
throne).

Not everyone can see the golden globe of Saturn
without a telescope. It is not much more than a point
of pearl-white light to the naked eye even in clear skies.
Some sharp-eyed astronomers say they can pick out
Uranus, but it is not classed as a naked-eye planet.
Neptune cannot be seen with the unaided eye at all and
is therefore eliminated as a possibility. Clouds shining
like gold zero in on Saturn. Jupiter is reddish. Uranus
looks blue-green. Neptune looks blue.

Since heaven is visible, that narrows our choices
down to Jupiter and Saturn. Of these, only Saturn has
golden clouds.

Traveling The Circuit of Heaven

The Lord's dwelling place orbits, suggesting that it
is a planet. Job 22:12–14 says,

Is not God in the height of heaven? . . . thou
sayest, How doth God know? can he judge
through the dark cloud? Thick clouds are a covering to him, that he seeth not; and **he walketh
in the circuit of heaven.**

His going forth is from the end (*qatsah;* extrem-
ity) of the heaven, and **his circuit** unto the ends
(extremities) of it.[45]

The circuit he travels is an important clue. Only planets, asteroids, or comets circle in front of the stationary
field of stars, which are too far away for us to see any

orbital movement at all during one man's lifetime. Only the most sophisticated equipment can determine that the stars are moving at all.

The Third Heaven

What is the third heaven? Paul spoke of paradise (where the tree of life is) as being the third heaven. He said,

> I knew a man in Christ . . . (whether in the body, I cannot tell; or whether out of the body, I cannot tell: God knoweth;) such an one caught up to the **third heaven**. . . . caught up into **paradise** (*paradeison,* an Eden).[46]

If paradise is in the third heaven, the first heaven would be Mars, the second Jupiter and the third Saturn. This tallies with other scriptures that place the Lord's throne in our solar system like the Sun, Moon and Earth, which are visible spheres. Psalm 78:69 says that the Lord

> **built his sanctuary like high palaces** (Green's Interlinear has 'places;' i.e., planets), **like the earth** (a planet) which he hath established for ever.

> His seed (Jesus) shall endure for ever, and his throne **as the sun** (a body in our solar system) before me. It shall be established for ever **as the moon** (another heavenly body in this solar system) and as **a faithful witness** (therefore visible) **in heaven.**[47]

The Morning Star

Concerning our heavenly home, Jesus said, "**I will give him** (the overcomer) **the morning star.**" This is perfect for **Saturn is a morning star** when I think the Rapture will take place—on Pentecost at the end of May in 1998.

On March 1, 1998, Saturn will go behind the moon, but that will not be visible here in California. After that, Saturn can be seen in the evening sky shining, with its steady light that barely flickers, low in the west in the constellation Pisces until the middle of March.

From then until September, the evening sky will be devoid of planets, an unusually long time. The morning sky before dawn will be spectacular and worth watching during April and May. You should be able to identify Saturn easily. Venus will be moving into conjunction with both Jupiter and Saturn. By April 23, Jupiter and Venus will appear to be in the same spot in Pisces. Saturn will be entering Aries.

After he said, "I will give him the morning star," Jesus added,

He that hath an ear, let him hear what the Spirit saith unto the churches (it sounds important).[48]

In Revelation 22:16, Jesus also said, "I am the root and the offspring of David, and **the bright and morning star**" (or resplendent morning star, as in the Concordant version). Why would he call himself the morning star unless it was to give us a clue to where his throne is located?

When Jesus was born in Bethlehem, wise men came from the east to Jerusalem, "Saying, Where is he that is born King of the Jews? for we have seen his star in the east, and are come to worship him.''[49] If his star is in the east, it fits right in with the other indications that his throne is considered to be east of Eden.

When Christ returns in glory, he is said to come out of the east. In the Olivet Discourse, Jesus said,

> For as the lightning cometh out of the east, and shineth even unto the west; so shall also the coming of the Son of man be.[50]

Our space exploration found a few thin faint rings around the other giant planets, but Saturn is the only planet marked with such a resplendent royal halo. The rings seem to be made up of chunks of actual water-ice crystals. Whether or not there are rocks in the center of each piece of ice is unknown at this time. The ring system is described as ''the likeness of an expanse like the sparkle of awesome ice.''[51]

Satan's original home was also a morning star. Any planet seen in the morning sky is a morning star.

Both of Satan's dwelling places in the heavenlies, the planet Rahab and the asteroid called Wormwood in Revelation 8:11, a broken piece of Rahab, orbit the Earth. Scripture says,

> How has Lucifer, **that rose in the morning** (or **shining star, son of the morning,** Green's Interlinear), fallen from heaven! He that sent orders to all the nations is **crushed to the earth.** But thou saidst in thine heart . . . I will be like the Most High (Isaiah 14:12–14, LXX).

(When) the angels of God came to stand before the Lord . . . the devil came with them. And the Lord said to the devil, Whence art thou come? And the devil . . . said, I am come from **compassing** (orbiting around) **the earth,** and walking up and down in the world (Job 1:6,7, KJV).

I have gone **round about the earth,** and walked through it (Job 1:7, Douay Version).

Seven Eyes on One Stone

Because "Joshua" from the Hebrew is the same as "Jesus" from the Greek, the English translation of the Greek Septuagint brings out the real meaning of Zechariah 3:1–10. This version makes it easy to recognize Jesus for who he really was.

And the Lord shewed me **Jesus the high priest** standing before the angel of the Lord, and the Devil stood on his right hand to resist him . . . If thou wilt walk in my ways, and take heed to my charges, then shalt thou judge my house: and if thou wilt diligently keep my court, then will I give thee men to walk in the midst of these that stand here. Hear now, **Jesus the high priest,** thou, and thy neighbors that are sitting before thee: for they are diviners (*mowpheth,* men who in their persons shadow forth future events[52]), for, behold, I bring forth my servant The Branch. For **as for the stone which I have set before the face of Jesus, on the one stone are seven eyes** (orbs).

It is perfect. This stone is number seven, and seven is God's number. These seven orbs, or spheres, could be diagramed as follows:

O O O O O O O

This seems like a celestial map indicating that the throne of Jesus will be on the seventh planet—Mercury, Venus, Earth, Mars, Rahab, Jupiter, then Saturn. We put a similar celestial map in our spaceships so someone could figure out that they came from the third planet from the sun.

O O Q O O͡ O O

The Lampstand

Just as God's prophecies can have a double reference, his symbols sometimes do double duty. The lampstand is one of these symbols.

The seven-branched golden lampstand in the tabernacle seems not only to represent Christ as the light of the world, but to indicate where his throne is located with respect to the Earth. Ezekiel said that the cherubim's appearance was as lamps.[53] In the golden lampstand, there were seven bowls and seven lamps in the bowls.

If the middle lamp represents Saturn, the three lamps on the left would represent Mars, which is next outside Earth's orbit, then Rahab and Jupiter. The three lamps on the right would represent Uranus, Neptune, and Pluto. It fits well for the sun only lights up the near side of each planet. From space, they actually do resemble spot lights in bowl-shaped fixtures. Also, the branches of the lampstand form quarter circles, suggesting orbits on either side of Saturn's.

When Solomon built the temple, he made ten lampstands and placed them in the Holy Place. Why ten? King David gave him the instructions for building the temple, and David said that he understood the works of the pattern. Also, Solomon was said to have had both wisdom and knowledge above other men. It was no accident that the ten lampstands echo the fact that there were originally ten cherubim. Second Chronicles 4:7 in the Jerusalem Bible says,

> He made the ten golden lamp-stands according to the pattern and placed them in the Hekal, **five on the right and five on the left.**

The Ten Curtains

Imagine standing in the middle of the tabernacle, looking up at the curtains that have cherubim embroidered on them. The five rear curtains on our left represent Mercury, Venus, Earth, Mars, and Rahab. The five front curtains on our right stand for Jupiter, Saturn, Uranus, Neptune, and Pluto. Both sets are hooked together unifying our planetary system.

When the ten curtains are spread over the supporting boards of the tabernacle, two and a half curtains hang down the back and seven and a half cover the top. Thus the one that folds over the upper back corner represents Earth and the rest of the top represents the same planets as the lampstand.

The symbolism of the tabernacle was carried over to the temple. When Ezekiel 9:3 in the Lamsa translation says that "the glory of the God of Israel was gone up from the cherub which stood on the **corner** of the house," the glory had gone up from the Earth. When Ezekiel 10:18 (Lamsa) mentions that "the glory of the LORD departed from the **corner** of the temple, and stood over the cherubim," we know that the glory departed from the Earth and stood above more than one planet.

This special identification of Earth with the corner is one reason why Psalm 118:22 says, "The stone which the builders refused is become the **head stone of the corner.**" Christ will be king over the Earth. Psalm 144:11,12 takes on new meaning. It says,

> Rid me, and deliver me from the hand of strange children (the catastrophe will do it) . . . that our daughters (Israelites during the Millennium) may be **as corner stones** (earthly leaders under Christ the King of kings and Lord of lords), polished (*chatab*, carved) after the similitude of a palace" (in a government set up on Earth, as it is in heaven).[54]

Evidently, the third, fifth and seventh planets were assigned respectively to Adam, Satan and the Lord Jesus Christ for their thrones. Satan, not content with just his own kingdom, took dominion away from Adam and tried to be "like the Most High." Yet, this hope of his is in vain, his time short. I believe the Satan-possessed False Prophet will lose his mitre and crown on the Feast of Trumpets, September 13, 2007.

Ash-Colored Horses

In Zechariah 6:1–8 in the LXX, the asteroids are aptly depicted as ash-colored horses. Many are clinkers. He said,

I . . . lifted up my eyes . . . (i.e., he looked up at the sky and saw) four chariots coming out from between two . . . brazen mountains. In the first chariot were red horses: and in the second chariot black horses, and in the third chariot white horses, and in the fourth chariot piebald and ash-colored horses. . . . These are the four winds (or spirits) of heaven, and they are going forth to stand before the Lord of all the earth.

FOUR "SPIRITS" OF THE HEAVENS
BETWEEN TWO BRAZEN MOUNTAINS
STANDING BEFORE THE LORD

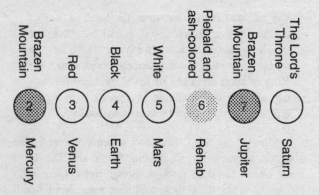

The ash-colored asteroids whip around the Earth

If the two brazen mountains are Mercury and Jupiter, the four chariots between them represent Venus, Earth, Mars, and Rahab, and they are all **before** the Lord's planet, Saturn. "And **the ash-coloured went out**," Zechariah continued, "and looked to go and compass the earth: and he said, **Go, and compass** (*shuwt*, whip around, i.e., orbit) **the earth.**'' These are the Near Earth Asteroids. Everything is set up.

A Sling and a Stone

This idea of whipping around brings to mind the story of David and Goliath, who defied the armies of Israel. David picked up five smooth stones out of the brook and put them in his shepherd's bag. He used one of these to whip around in his leather sling. When he let go of one thong, the rock flew out and hit the giant Goliath in the forehead. ''So David prevailed over the Philistine with a sling and with a stone.''[55]

David represented Christ, the Son of David, and Goliath represented the great army that will attack Israel at the end of the Tribulation. This giant will also be stopped with a slingstone. A whirlwind will whip it around and sling it into the Earth. The Son of David will also prevail with a sling and a stone.

Rescue is Available

Since there is a way of leaving here before the NEA called Wormwood[56] destroys civilization, we should take it. Jesus is willing to rescue you if you trust him. Ask him to be your Saviour. Hebrews 2:3 asks, ''How shall we escape (just recompense), if we neglect so great salvation?'' There are two Raptures when Jesus will gather his believers and take them to heaven. The first is described in I Thessalonians 4:16,17:

(The) Lord himself shall descend from heaven with a shout, with the voice of the archangel, and with the trump of God: and the dead **in Christ** shall rise first: Then we which are alive and remain shall be **caught up** together with them in

the clouds, to meet the Lord in the air: and so
shall we ever be with the Lord.

Jesus Christ promised,

> "Because thou hast kept the word of my patience,
> I also will keep thee from the hour of temptation
> (which is the seven-year Tribulation), which shall
> come upon all the world, to try them that dwell
> upon the earth."[57]

Many Will See The Rapture

It came as a great surprise to me, but it looks like
many people will actually see the Rapture take place,
be filled with awe, and trust in the Lord. Psalm 40:1–3
in the New English Bible says,

> I waited, waited for the LORD (as the Philadel-
> phians are patiently waiting in Revelation 3:10), he
> bent down to me and heard my cry. **He brought
> me up** out of the muddy pit, out of the mire (out
> of the Earth) and the clay (our bodies of clay); he
> set my feet on a rock (the heavenly planet) and
> gave me firm footing; and on my lips he put **a new
> song** (sung after the Rapture[58]), a song of praise to
> our God. **Many when they see will be filled with
> awe and will learn to trust in the LORD.**

The King James Version has "many shall see it, and
fear, and shall trust in the LORD." The message is
consistent in other versions; compare the NIV, RSV,
Berkeley, New Jerusalem, Amplified, Lamsa, and Confraternity. Contrary to what we have been taught about

a secret Rapture, many will see us taken up in the Rapture and will believe in Christ. God never leaves himself without a witness in the world.

Saved so As by Fire

At Rapture II, they will be "saved; yet so as by fire."[59] They will just barely escape before the Arrow of the Lord's Deliverance hits Earth. Scripture says,

> The LORD thundered from heaven . . . he sent out arrows . . . the channels of the sea appeared, the foundations of the world were discovered, at the rebuking of the LORD, at the blast of the breath of his nostrils. **He sent from above, he took me;** he drew me out of many waters (nations); He delivered me . . . in the day of my calamity (the day of Jacob's trouble[60]) . . . **He brought me forth also into a large place** (a giant planet).[61]

> For in the time of trouble (just before the asteroid impact as this age ends and the Millennium begins) **he shall hide me in his pavilion** (in heaven): **in the secret of his tabernacle** (which reveals where heaven is located) **shall he hide me;** he shall **set me up upon a rock** (planet, i.e., Saturn).[62]

> These are they which came out of great tribulation, and have washed their robes, and made them white in the blood of the Lamb. Therefore are they before the throne of God, and serve him day and night in his temple: and he that sitteth on the throne shall dwell among them. They shall hunger no more, neither thirst any more; neither shall the sun light on them (because of the thick golden clouds) nor any

heat (*kauma,* consuming heat), For the Lamb which is in the midst of the throne shall feed them, and shall lead them unto living fountains of waters: and God shall wipe away all tears.[63]

There is More to it Than This

It looks to me like Saturn is heaven, where neither moth nor rust doth corrupt, and thieves do not break through and steal. Nothing will ever be allowed to defile the "sapphire" planet. That is why **Sapphira** died when she lied to the Spirit of the Lord.[64] She was made an example.

In the Lord Jesus Christ "dwelleth all the fulness of the Godhead bodily,"[65] but Scripture tells us that God cannot be contained in one place, not even on the "sapphire" throne. The Lord was present in the earthly tabernacle and will sit on the throne of David on Earth at his Second Advent. He will sit on his throne in our heaven, but there is more to it than this.

The universe is enormous, and "All things were made by him."[66] God is spirit.[67] "For in him we live, and move, and have our being."[68] There is also a heaven of heavens, but in I Kings 8:27, Solomon said that "the heaven and heaven of heavens cannot contain thee." However, "the heaven and the heaven of heavens is the LORD'S thy God, the earth also."[69]

We cannot see him. "No man hath seen God at any time; the only begotten Son, which is in the bosom of the Father, he hath declared him."[70]

It always was the Son of God who dealt with mankind, in the Old Testament as Yahweh (the pre-incarnate Christ) and as the angel of the Lord. Then as Y'shua (Greek, Iesous), Jesus (the incarnate Christ), in the New Testament, he gave the invisible bodily form and substance.

He was both man and God, Emmanuel, God with us. The name Jesus means Yahweh is Saviour. When we get to heaven, we will see him as he is. However, even there, we will still see God in the face of the Lord Jesus Christ.

Referring to the heavenly New Jerusalem, John wrote that

> the throne (one throne) of God and of the Lamb shall be in it: and his servants shall serve him (one person, both God and the Lamb): And they shall see his face (one face)'' and his name (one name) shall be in their foreheads. And there shall be no night there; and they need no candle, neither light of the sun (it's far from the sun, but we won't need it); for the Lord God giveth them light.[71]

Heaven is the Pearl of Great Price

Between 1994 and 1996, Saturn's rings will present themselves to us edge-on and seem to disappear. Then, Saturn will hang there like a great pearl in the sky, revealing the meaning of the parable of the pearl of great price. Jesus said,

> the **kingdom of heaven** is like unto a merchant man, seeking goodly pearls: Who, when he had found one **pearl of great price,** went and sold all that he had, and bought it.[72]

The Lord's Throne in Heaven

Many clues indicate that the Lord's throne is on Saturn, originally the seventh planet from the sun but now the sixth because Satan's planet Rahab was split into relatively small pieces. The "paradise of God" is in "the third heaven" on a pearl-like heavenly body in our solar system, "as the sun," "as the moon," and "like the earth."

It has beautiful "clouds shining like gold" and a resplendent halo befitting the palace of deity, the King of kings and Lord of lords. HALOed be His Name. While effectively shielding his great brightness from us, Saturn still "shines afar off in the heavens" "as a faithful witness in heaven" and is inexplicably known by our astronomers to radiate three times more heat than it receives from the sun.

Remember that the place Jesus is preparing for us is marked off from the surrounding space? Saturn's place is marked off from the surrounding space by it's magnificent halo of ice crystals.

That is perfect. Heaven has a halo. You need magnification of at least 40 to see it though. The heavens do declare the glory of God. In heaven, Christ shines with glory and his place shines with the likeness of his glory. Ezekiel described the scene:

And above the firmament (the expanse of space) that was over their heads (i.e., farther out in space than the terrestrial planets) was the likeness of a throne, as the appearance of a sapphire stone: and upon the likeness of the throne was the likeness as the appearance of a man (the Lord Jesus Christ) above upon it. And I saw as the colour of amber (Saturn's golden clouds), as the appearance of fire round about within it (heaven), from the appearance of his loins (*mothen,* waist, i.e., from its equator) even upward, and from the appearance of his loins (from its equator) even downward, I saw as it were the appearance of fire, and it had brightness round about (i.e., the ring system). As the appearance of **the bow** that is in the cloud in the day of rain (the rainbow caused by the sun shining on the ice crystals), so was the appearance of the brightness round about. **This** (the brightness and beautiful colors of the rainbow) **was the appearance of the likeness of the glory of the LORD.**[73]

God came from Ternan (which means perfect, a country to the east), and the Holy One from mount Paran (beauty, glory, ornament, abounding in foliage). Selah (which means stop and think about that). **His glory covered the heavens.**[74]

Saturn is the perfect country placed to the east on our celestial map. It is easily the Lord's most beautiful ornament in the solar system. It is the slowest of the naked-eye planets and always travels on the ecliptic, the apparent path of the sun through the constellations.

A Levitical city also suggests Saturn and her ring system. See the diagram printed in Unger's Bible Dictionary. The central city itself was round. Then outside there were suburbs surrounding the city, then fields and vineyards around that.

The Levites were the priestly tribe. As a type of heaven, the Levitical city is a good one. It was a city of refuge, and Hebrews 6:18 refers to heaven as a refuge.

Jesus Christ, our High Priest within the veil "of the true tabernacle, which the Lord pitched, and not man"[75] assures us that we will go there also. We are to be with him where he is.[76] Within the veil represents heaven. Hebrews 6:18–20 says for us

A LEVITICAL CITY

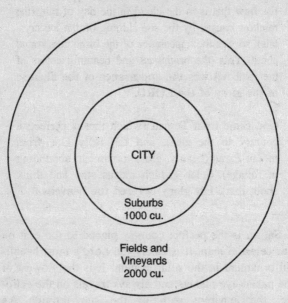

CITY

Suburbs
1000 cu.

Fields and
Vineyards
2000 cu.

who have fled for refuge to lay hold upon the
hope set before us (the hope of heaven): Which
hope we have as an anchor of the soul, both sure
and stedfast, and which entereth into that within
the veil (heaven); Whither the forerunner is for
us entered, even Jesus (who ascended to heaven),
made an high priest for ever after the order of
Melchisedec ('a priest continually'[77]).

5 ✣ *The Tabernacle Pattern*

THE TABERNACLE CONTAINS MORE ASTONISHING secrets. Certainly, many things about it have to do with Christ. He is the light of the world and the bread of life. His flesh was torn like the veil to atone for the sins of the world and to open the door of heaven for us. However, so much emphasis has been placed on this aspect that the other meanings of the various parts of the tabernacle have been slighted.

Symbolic Model of the Heavens

Hebrews 9:23,24 tells us plainly that the tabernacle and its apparatus are "patterns of things in the heavens . . . figures of the true." Therefore, they are symbols that stand for real things in the heavens.

The symbols are in the first diagram on the following page. Think about what they could represent in the heavens before you examine the second diagram closely. The easiest to see is that the Holy of Holies represents the physical location of heaven where the throne of the Lord is. The Lord said,

> I will commune with thee from **above** the mercy seat, from between the two cherubims.[1]

Heaven is between two cherubim, or planets, farther out on space than the Asteroid Belt, represented by the stones in the Ark. The Talmud says that both the whole

"PATTERNS OF THINGS IN THE HEAVENS"

THINGS IN THE HEAVENS

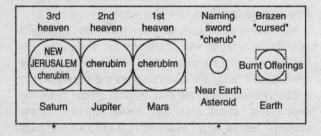

"his throne"   "the hammer of the whole earth," Jer. 50:23
House of the Lord   "the curse that goeth forth over the
our "place," Jn. 14:2   face of the whole earth," Zech. 5:3

tablets and the ones that Moses broke because the Israelites made a golden calf were put in the Ark,[2] suggesting the split rocks we call asteroids.

The interpretation presented in the diagram on page 140 squares with Scripture and with our solar system. Second Corinthians 12:2 tells us that Paul "knew a man in Christ . . . caught up to the **third heaven.**" Therefore, the place that men who are believers are going to be caught up to is the third heaven.

We are to be with Christ, so he is also in the third heaven. Where he is, his throne is. So his throne is in the third heaven.

If we could step from one planet to the next, from Earth, the next stepping stone would be Mars. The second would be Jupiter. The third step would put us directly on Saturn, the third heaven. Since Christ is in the third heaven, it seems that his throne is on Saturn.

The Throne and The Footstool

From Revelation 21:10, we find out that this place we are heading for is called New Jerusalem. Just as Jerusalem is on the rock we call Earth, I believe New Jerusalem is on the third heavenly rock called Saturn.

The Lord said, "The heaven is my throne, and the earth is my footstool."[3] Therefore, it makes sense that heaven, the throne, would be larger than Earth, the footstool. It also seems that Earth would be placed in front of and not too far away from the throne. On our celestial map, in front of would mean closer to the sun.

Saturn is larger than Earth. The giant planet's diameter is 74,600 miles. Earth's diameter is only 7,926 miles, and it is closer to the sun than Saturn.

EARTH: THE LORD'S FOOTSTOOL

Sun   Mercury   Venus   Earth   Mars   Astroid Belt   Jupiter   Saturn

King David Reinstated

The heavenly New Jerusalem is "the throne of God and of the Lamb,"[4] and the earthly Jerusalem is "the throne of David."[5] Christ will sit on both. He will sit on the throne of David while setting up the Millennial government. Then he will put David back on his own throne and return to his heavenly home. He says that in those days,

> they shall serve the LORD their God, and David their king, whom I will raise up unto them.[6]

> And I the LORD will be their God, and my servant David a prince among them; I the LORD have spoken it.[7]

Altar of Earth

Right after the Lord gave Moses the Ten Commandments, he said, "An **altar of earth** thou shalt make unto me."[8] Therefore, Earth is equated with an altar. You can see this as you read Isaiah 27:9; 28:13. When the flaming sword shooteth forth,

> By this therefore shall the iniquity of Jacob be purged; and this is all the fruit to take away his

sin; when he maketh all **the stones of the altar as chalkstones** that are beaten in sunder, the groves and images shall not stand. . . . And it shall come to pass in that day, that the LORD shall beat off (*chabat,* thresh, beat out as with a stick) from the channel of the river (Euphrates) unto the stream of Egypt, . . . And it shall come to pass in that day, that the **great trumpet** shall be blown.

Egypt will not be inhabited from the tower of Syene to the border of Ethiopia for the next 40 years[9] It will happen when the *Tekiah Gedolah,* the Great Trumpet that is blown on the Feast of Trumpets, sounds.

The Curse and The Cross Hairs

The last verse of the Old Testament ends with ''lest I come and smite the earth with a curse.'' According to Zechariah 5:3, the curse ''goeth forth over the face of the whole earth,'' so the curse orbits all around this globe.

It is to strike Earth at Babylon on the Euphrates River and destroy her by burning[10] Also, the altar of burnt offering in the tabernacle was brass, a symbol of a curse. Therefore, the brazen altar of burnt offerings not only fits Earth, but it is as if the literal city of Babylon were centered directly on the main crosspieces of the grate, like cross hairs on a bombsight.

Ground Zero

This reminds us that the astronomical symbol of Earth is a circle divided into quarters, and the point of the sword is set against Babylon.

I have set the point of the sword against all their gates, that their heart may faint, and their ruins be multiplied: ah! it is made bright, it is wrapped up (sharpened) for the slaughter.[11]

The Burnt Offering

When the tabernacle was set up and the sacrificing commenced, the Lord said,

Now this is that which thou shalt offer upon the altar; **two lambs** of the first year day by day continually. The one lamb thou shalt offer in the morning; and the other lamb thou shalt offer at even.[12]

Why were there two lambs sacrificed continually? Christ is the Lamb of God that was our Passover.[13] He was sacrificed in the morning of this Church Age, and he died "once . . . to put away sin by the sacrifice of himself."[14] The second lamb could not stand for another sacrifice of Christ in the evening of this age. The two lambs either stand for Christ being put on the cross in the morning and dying "between the evenings," between 3:00 and 5:00 P.M., on Crucifixion Day, or the second lamb stands for the burnt offering at the end of the age, when the curse strikes the Earth.

Zephaniah might help us understand. Whether the second lamb has anything to do with it or not, the Lord has also prepared a sacrifice. It is to take place on the Feast of Trumpets, right after this age ends. Zephaniah said,

> **The day of the LORD** is at hand: for the LORD hath prepared a sacrifice. . . . And it shall come to pass in the **day of the LORD'S sacrifice,** that I will punish the princes, and the king's children, and all such as are clothed with strange apparel. . . . there shall be . . . a great crashing from the hills. . . . That day is **a day of wrath,** a day of trouble and distress, a day of wasteness and desolation, a day of . . . thick darkness, A **day of the trumpet** and alarm against the fenced cities, and against the high towers (the world church and government).[15]

The Brass Laver For Cleansing

The round Laver was also brass for it stood for the curse that would cleanse Earth. Because it was placed between the Brazen Altar (Earth) and the tabernacle proper (the three heavens), it is probably a Near Earth Asteroid.

The NEAs do orbit out farther than the first heaven, but the planets orbit too and they are still diagramed as if all lined up in a straight line.

Satan's Key

The asteroid called Wormwood is the key that will open hell, and this key was given to Satan, also called Lucifer.

AND the fifth angel sounded, and I saw a star (i.e., Lucifer, which means morning star) fall (fallen) from heaven unto the earth: and **to him was given the key of the bottomless pit.** And he opened the bottomless pit.[16]

From Heaven to The Recesses of The Pit

Satan wanted to ascend to heaven and be like the Most High. However, his hopes are in vain. He will be cast out of heaven, cut down to the Earth, and finally chained in the bottomless pit for 1,000 years. Isaiah 14 helps us understand his aspirations, his fall, and his trip to the dark underground dungeon. He is to be cut down to the Earth Mid-Tribulation and be put in the dungeon after he loses the battle of Armageddon.

How you have fallen from heaven, O star of the morning (Lucifer, in the KJV), son of the dawn! You have been cut down to the earth . . . you said in your heart, I will ascend to heaven (from his station below heaven); I will raise my throne above the stars of God, And I will sit on the mount of assembly (where the church will assemble at the Rapture) In the recesses of the north. I will ascend above the heights of the clouds (i.e., the golden clouds); I will make myself like the Most High (Christ). Nevertheless you will be

The Tabernacle Pattern 147

thrust down to Sheol, To the recesses of the pit (Isaiah 14:12–15, NASB).

Satan's Nest Among The Stars

After his planet Rahab was hit with a rock and split into pieces, Satan made his habitation on a chunk of it that was thrown out into a cometary orbit by the impact explosion. His nest among the stars is described in Obadiah 1:3,4, where the Lord goes beyond Edom (which means red, Satan's color) and addresses Satan himself:

The pride of thine heart hath deceived thee, thou that dwellest in the clefts of the rock, whose habitation is high; that saith in his heart, Who shall bring me down to the ground? Though thou exalt thyself as the eagle, and though thou set thy nest among the stars, thence will I bring thee down, saith the LORD.

The Sword of The Lord

The curse is also called the Sword of the Lord. In Isaiah 34:5, the Lord said, "my sword (*chereb*) shall be bathed in heaven." Therefore, the Laver represented something in the heavenlies. It is the "flaming sword" of Genesis 3:24, placed in the sky to guard the pathway leading to the third heaven. It is to keep the evil that has come to a head on Earth from invading heaven.

The Face-Bread

The Table of Shewbread, or Showbread (*shulhan lehem panim,* table of the face), had twelve loaves of unleavened bread (literally, face-bread) on it. Christ said,

> For the bread of God is he which cometh down
> from heaven and giveth life unto the world . . .
> I am the bread of life: he that cometh to me shall
> never hunger.[17]

The fact that there were twelve loaves shows us that this table of the face indicated that Christ would show his face to the twelve tribes of Israel. This tallies with Jesus' statement in Matthew 15:24: "I am not sent but unto the lost sheep of the house of Israel." Jesus showed his face to Israel.

Altar of Incense: Prayers of Saints

The Golden Altar of Incense was placed right at the veil that represented his flesh,[18] and the door to the third heaven, which is Christ's throne. The veil itself had cherubim embroidered on it, furnishing us another clue that he lived on a cherubim. Blood was put on the Mercy Seat and on the horns of the Golden Altar of Incense to represent Jesus' blood that was shed to atone for the sins of the world, for "without shedding of blood is no remission."[19]

> And Aaron shall burn thereon sweet incense every
> morning . . . And when Aaron **lighteth the lamps
> at even,** he shall burn incense upon it . . . And
> Aaron shall make an atonement upon the horns
> of it once in a year with the blood of the sin-
> offering of atonements.[20]

In Revelation 8:3, we find that the incense represents the prayers of all the saints: "and there was given unto him much incense, that he should offer it with the prayers of all saints upon the golden altar which was before the throne."

The Pay-Back

Remember that the Lord said, "Vengeance is mine. I will repay."[21] These prayers are the cries the saints poured out to the Lord because of the many injustices done to them, including burning at the stake, throwing them to the lions, crucifying them, etc. The pay-back is coming, and it will be twice as bad as the disaster that destroyed Sodom and Gomorrah.

> Reward her (Babylon) even as she rewarded you, and **double** unto her **double** according to her works: in the cup which she hath filled fill to her **double**.[22]

> Be not a terror unto me: thou art my hope in the day of evil. . . . bring upon them the day of evil, and destroy them with **double destruction**.[23]

The Globe Thrown at The Altar of Earth

The prayers and smoke of incense "ascended up before God . . . And the angel took the censer, and filled it with fire of the altar, and cast it into the earth: and there were voices, and thunderings, and lightnings, and an earthquake."[24] This globe shaped censer represents the asteroid crashing into the altar of the Earth.

To depict this, Numbers 16:32–38 tells us that when Korah, Dathan and Abiram (which means father of fraud) gathered a group together against Moses and Aaron,

> the earth opened her mouth, and swallowed them up . . . They . . . went down alive into the pit, and the earth closed upon them . . . And there came out a fire from the LORD, and consumed the two hundred and fifty men that offered incense. And the LORD spoke unto Moses, saying, Speak unto Eleazar the son of Aaron the priest, that he take up the censers out of the burning, and scatter thou the fire yonder; for they are hallowed. The **censers** of these sinners against their own souls, let them **make them broad plates for a covering of the altar** . . . and they shall be **a sign** unto the children of Israel.

The censers represent rocks cast down to the altar of the Earth, and there were 250 of them. Revelation 16:21 shows that these rocks will weigh around 100 pounds each. It says, "And there fell upon men a great hail out of heaven, every stone about the weight of a talent."

Earth Turned Upside Down

The pieces of the comet, or asteroid, that just struck Jupiter is a demonstration of things to come on Earth at the end of this age. You don't want to be here then. The Earth will be knocked upside down:

> BEHOLD, the LORD maketh the earth empty, and maketh it waste, and **turneth it upside down,** and scattereth abroad the inhabitants.[25]

There will be a world-wide earthquake. Like the wall of Jericho, every wall will fall.[26] Jesus will save you, but you have to believe in him or take the consequences. Make up your mind. Time is short. This could happen in your lifetime.

The asteroid will be cast down to Earth right after Christ receives his crown in heaven. "THE LORD reigneth . . . he sitteth between the cherubims (planets); **let the earth be moved.**"[27]

The golden censer, which directs when the asteroid will strike, belongs to the third heaven, "the Holiest of all," which represents Christ's golden-cloud-wrapped planetary throne. Heb. 9:2–5 says,

> There was a tabernacle made; the first, wherein was the candlestick, and the table, and the shewbread; which is called the sanctuary (*hagia,* Holy Place). And after the second veil, the tabernacle which is called **the Holiest of all** (i.e., heaven); **Which had the golden censer,** and the ark of the covenant overlaid round about with gold, wherein was the golden pot that had manna (angel's food,[28]), and Aaron's rod that budded, and the tables of the covenant; And over it the cherubims of glory shadowing the mercyseat.

When the censer is thrown down the rock will be removed out of its place. Job 18:4,5,10,15 tells us that

> He teareth himself in his anger . . . and **shall the rock be removed out of his place? Yea,** the light of the wicked (the False Prophet) shall be put out . . . The snare is laid for him in the ground, and a trap for him in the way (in his path in space). . . . His confidence shall be rooted out of his tabernacle, and it shall bring him to **the king of terrors.** It shall dwell in his tabernacle, be-

cause it is none of his (he has stolen the church[29]): brimstone shall be scattered upon his habitation.

The Star of God

The Lord "stretcheth out the heavens as a curtain, and spreadeth them out as a tent to dwell in."[30] There were ten tabernacle curtains. Each one represented one planet in our solar system. As the planets are lit in our night sky, the lamps on the lampstand were lit in the evening.[31] They too represented planets. This is why the lampstand was made of beaten gold. The planets were all formed by coalescence.

This diagram shows which planets are represented by the curtains and lampstand. They point to "Chiun (Kiyuwn, Saturn) . . . **THE STAR OF YOUR GOD**" (Amos 5:26, emphasis mine).

Images of Heaven Forbidden

The Israelites went into captivity for making an image of Saturn to worship it. Beware of making images, those we might make are strictly forbidden. God has furnished us the tabernacle as a similitude of the heavens. It has the only images of these things we are to have. One of the commandments is:

> Thou shalt not make unto thee any graven image, **or any likeness of any thing that is in heaven above,** or that is in the earth beneath, or that is in the water under the earth.[32]

We are to worship God, not the planet where he set up his throne. Be careful. Maybe this is why this information did not come out sooner. Be sure to obey this commandment.

Ten Curtains and The Lampstand

A picture is said to be worth a thousand words. I think it may be true in this case. The following diagram can probably be understood much quicker than my words.

THE TABERNACLE CURTAINS
AND THE LAMPSTAND

Ten Curtains

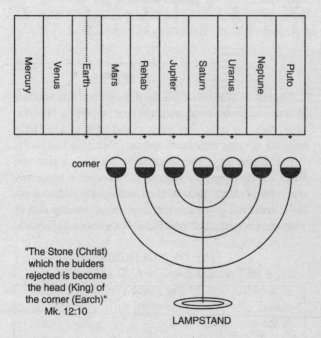

| Mercury | Venus | Earth | Mars | Rehab | Jupiter | Saturn | Uranus | Neptune | Pluto |

corner

"The Stone (Christ) which the buiders rejected is become the head (King) of the corner (Earch)" Mk. 12:10

LAMPSTAND

The seven cherubim east of Eden represent the same seven planets that the Lampstand represents. Also, the five cherubim flung from God's left hand and the five cherubim flung from God's right hand represent the same ten planets that the Tabernacle curtains represent. The Bible is consistent.

CURTAIN AND LAMPSTAND PARALLELS

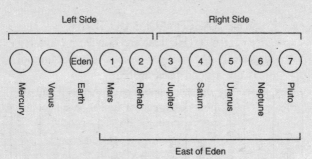

Left Side   Right Side

Eden 1 2 3 4 5 6 7

Mercury · Venus · Earth · Mars · Rehab · Jupiter · Saturn · Uranus · Neptune · Pluto

East of Eden

Genesis 3:24 showed that he placed cherubim (plural) between Eden on Earth and the Tree of Life in Heaven. From that, we knew that there would have to be at least two. As it turns out, there are two, Mars and Jupiter.

Rahab may have split apart about the time a piece hit Earth and destroyed the dinosaurs. Whenever it happened, one side of Mars took a good walloping. Astronomers have wondered why there are more craters on one side of Mars than on the other side. Rahab's explosion explains it.

THE TWO CERUBIM
BETWEEN EARTH AND HEAVEN

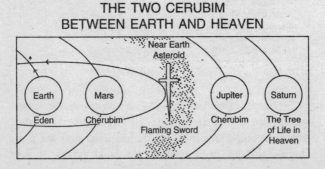

Near Earth Asteroid

Earth — Eden   Mars — Cherubim   Flaming Sword   Jupiter — Cherubim   Saturn — The Tree of Life in Heaven

Come Out of Her

The Lord drove Adam and Eve out of the Garden of Eden. Construction on the Tower of Babel was stopped by the Lord's intervention. Nebuchadnezzar's Babylon was done away with over time. Jesus said regarding today's Babylon, "Come out of her, my people, that ye be not partakers of her sins, and that ye receive not of her plagues."[33] Do you get the idea that that area of the Earth is not a good place to be?

That ground is cursed,[34] and The Curse will fall on it as the Millennium commences. It is not far in the future. Knowledge of what is coming is vital now.

> For this is the day of the Lord GOD of hosts, a day of vengeance, that he may avenge him of his adversaries: and **the sword** (*chereb*) shall devour, and it shall be satiate and made drunk with their blood: for the Lord GOD of hosts hath a sacrifice in the north country by the river Euphrates."[35]

THE FLAMING "CHEREB"

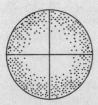

Knowing Where it is Won't Get You There

It is interesting to find out where our heaven is, but it is more important to understand the nature of our God. It doesn't help to know where heaven is if you can't get there. Along with Paul, I want all our hearts to be knit together in God's love and "unto all riches of the full assurance of understanding, to the acknowledgement of the mystery of God, and of the Father, and of Christ; In whom are hid all the treasures of wisdom and knowledge."[36]

It is important that we believe that Jesus is God and that he died and rose again.

And he said unto them, Ye are from beneath (below heaven): **I am from above** (farther out in space than the Earth): ye are of this world; **I am not of this world.** I said therefore unto you, that ye shall die in your sins: for **IF YE BELIEVE NOT THAT I AM HE,** (the Father) **YE SHALL DIE IN YOUR SINS**. . . . They understood not that he spake to them of the Father. Then said Jesus unto them, When ye have lifted up the Son of man, then shall ye know that **I AM HE** (the Father).[37] (All emphasis is mine.)

Jesus Christ is more than the babe in the manger, more than a good teacher, more than a healer, more than a prophet, although he was all of these. He is God himself in the human body of Jesus, the Son of God.

Those that have the Son have eternal life. Those who do not have the Son do not have eternal life.

And this is the record, that God hath given to us eternal life, and this life is in his Son. He that hath the Son hath life: and he that hath not the Son of God hath not life. . . . And we know that the Son of God is come, and hath given us an understanding, that we may know him that is true, and we are in him that is true, even in his Son **Jesus Christ. This is the true God,** and eternal life.[38]

We must believe that Jesus died and rose again to participate in the Rapture.

For **IF** we believe that Jesus died **and rose again** . . . Then we which are alive and remain shall be caught up together (this is the Rapture) with them in the clouds, to meet the Lord in the air: and so shall we ever be with the Lord.[39]

We must confess him with our mouth and believe it in our hearts to receive the free gift of the salvation of our souls.

IF thou shalt confess with thy mouth the Lord Jesus, and shalt believe in thine heart that God hath **raised him from the dead,** thou shalt be saved.[40]

There is no other name other than Jesus Christ by which we may be saved. God decided how men were to be saved before Adam was put on Earth. We have no say in the matter whatsoever. God is the sovereign of the universe. We must obey him.

It is simple. Either we do things his way or fail to make it to heaven, and "God was in Christ reconciling the world unto himself."[41] His word says,

Neither is there salvation in any other for there is none other name under heaven given among men, whereby we must be saved.[42]

Thus saith the LORD (Yahweh) the King of Israel, and his redeemer (Christ) the LORD (Yahweh) of hosts; **I am the first, and I am the last;** and beside me there is no God.[43]

Jesus Christ . . . I am Alpha and Omega, the beginning and the ending, saith the Lord, which is (at the Rapture), and which was (at the First Advent), and which is to come (at the Second Advent), **the Almighty.**[44]

Be ready for the Rapture. In the last chapter in the Bible, Jesus says,

I come quickly; and my reward is with me, to give every man according as his work shall be. I am Alpha and Omega, the beginning and the end, **the first** (Yahweh) **and the last** (Jesus Christ). Blessed are they that do his commandments, that they may have right to the tree of life, and may enter in through the gates (pearls) into the city.[45]

These pearly gates are to show that New Jerusalem is on the planet designated as the pearl of great price.

This New Jerusalem is in the heavenly **Sion,** which seems to be on the planet Saturn. Since it is shrouded in golden clouds, it is no wonder that when John saw it, "the street of the city was pure gold, as it were transparent glass."[46]

Symbols of heaven are gold, because it is the dwelling place of deity and is swathed in golden clouds, and the number seven, because it is the throne of our perfect Lord and is the seventh planet in our solar system. It is also symbolized by the sapphire because sapphire means Saturn and dear. It is Paradise, and it is attainable.

Free Ticket to The Morning Star

Saturn seems to be the morning star promised to over-comers in Revelation 2:28. If you are like me, you may want to see if you can pick it out in the sky. It should be easy to see during the month preceding the Rapture.

If you look at the eastern sky just before dawn on April 23, 1998, you should be able to see the bright conjuction of Venus and Jupiter. They should appear in just about the same spot. Venus is the brightest planet in the sky, Jupiter the second brightest. Saturn will just be rising. All three will be in the constellation Pisces.

If you look at them again on other mornings scattered throughout May, you will see Venus move away from Jupiter and head toward Saturn, which at the end of that period will be entering Aries, the Ram, a

THE MORNING STAR

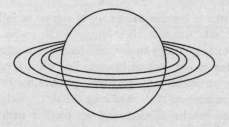

symbol of the Lamb of God. As the days go by, the whole scene will rotate into a better viewing position.

Now that you know your destination and how to get there, be sure you collect your free ticket for the trip of your life. If I am right, the Rapture is not far off.

Pray now if you never have. Tell Christ you accept him as your own personal Saviour. Don't get left behind.

All Things are Foretold

Jesus told us in Mark 13:23 and Matthew 10:26,

But take ye heed: behold, **I have foretold you all things.**

there is **nothing** covered, that shall not be revealed; and hid, that shall not be known.

Strong Meat for Those of Full Age

All can be revealed now because the Rapture is near. Take heed how you hear. Be teachers. Don't be a babe when actually of full age. The church is now old and can understand her strong meat.

Christ . . . became the author of eternal salvation unto all them that obey him . . . Of whom we have many things to say, and hard to be uttered, seeing ye are dull of hearing. For when for the time **ye ought to be teachers,** ye have need that one teach you again which be the first principles of the oracles of God; and are become such as have need of milk, and not of strong meat. For every one that useth milk is unskilful in the word of righteousness: for he is a babe. But **strong meat belongeth to them that are of full age** (today), even those who by reason of use have their senses exercised to discern both good and evil.[47]

6 ✢ The Morning Star: Christ's Throne

THE MOST GLORIOUS CORONATION CEREMONY OF all will be held in heaven on the Feast of Trumpets. At that time, Christ will receive a golden crown.

More important things happen on "that day" than any other day—ever—both good and bad.

> Alas! for **that day** is great, so that **none is like it:** it is even the time of Jacob's trouble, but he shall be saved out of it.[1]

Jesus Christ's throne is in heaven, and it is there that he will be crowned. By the time he returns to Earth, he has many crowns and already is the great "KING OF KINGS, AND LORD OF LORDS."[2]

Both the Old Testament saints and the church saints will be present at the coronation ceremony. Jesus Christ will be awarded the golden crown, glory, a kingdom and dominion over the Earth. What is his by right of creation is his also by right of redemption. His appointment as judge will also be confirmed[3] on that Feast of Trumpets.

> God mounts his throne amid shouts of joy; the LORD, amid **trumpet blasts.** Sing praise to God, sing praise, sing praise to our king, sing praise (Psalms 47:4, NAB).

The 21st Psalm in the New Jerusalem Bible is labeled, ''For a coronation ceremony. ''It goes beyond king David and shows that the joyous coronation of Christ in heaven and the devastating catastrophic asteroid impact on Earth take place on the same day.

> Yahweh, the king rejoices in your power . . . you come to meet him with blessings of prosperity, **put a crown of pure gold on his head**. . . . you invest him with splendour and majesty. You confer on him everlasting blessings . . . Your hand will reach all your enemies, your right hand all who hate you. **You will hurl them into a blazing furnace on the day when you appear** (the Sign of the Son of Man seen in heaven[4]); **Yahweh will engulf them in his anger,** and fire will devour them. You will purge the earth of their descendants . . . They have devised evil against you but, plot as they may, they will not succeed, since **you will make them turn tail, by shooting your arrows** in their faces. Rise, Yahweh, in your power! We will sing and make music in honour of your strength.

Just as Ahasuerus (which means chief) was already king before Esther (which means hidden, secret, or star) became queen, the Marriage of the Lamb will take place after Christ receives his crown. The Bride of Christ will be joint-heirs with him.

After the wedding ceremony, the last trump will sound for the saved and call the Tribulation saints to the Marriage Supper of the Lamb.[5] At this reception, the Church saints are the bride. The Tribulation saints are the friends of the bride, and the Old Testament saints are the friends of the bride-groom.[6]

That Feast of Trumpets is also the day of the Judgment Seat of Christ. After the arrival of the Tribulation saints in heaven, he will reward all the saints in heaven for their belief and at the same time pour out the just rewards for unbelief on those left on Earth. It is also the Day of God's Wrath,[7] the day of destruction, and the time of the vengeance of his temple.

See *Exit: 2007, The Secret of Secrets* for more details on the many events of the first day of the millennial Day of the Lord. Christ was born on the Feast of Trumpets and will be crowned on his birthday, Tishri 1, as the Millennium begins.

He will return to Earth soon afterward, but not immediately. There is a gap of seven months[8] between the Day of God's Wrath and the Second Advent of Christ. During this time, the Earth regains its equilibrium, the dust of destruction clears away. and Israel buries the dead to cleanse the land.

Judgment of the Nations

Soon after he arrives will be another phase of judgment, the Judgment of the Nations, when he will separate the sheep from the goats. The sheep will inherit the millennial kingdom. To the goats, he will say, "Depart from me, ye cursed, into everlasting fire, prepared for the devil and his angels."[9]

Armageddon

Some people misunderstand when the battle of Armageddon is to take place. It cannot take place before Christ literally puts his feet on the Earth. Revelation 19:19 shows that he is present when Armageddon is fought. John said,

> I saw the beast, and the kings of the earth, and their armies, gathered together to make war against him (Christ) that sat on the horse, and against his army (the saints).

As soon as dominion is taken away from Satan, the battle of Armageddon will be fought, and Christ will prevail.[10] At its end, the Beast and False Prophet will be cast into the Lake of Fire and Satan will be chained for a thousand years.[11] From that time on, the peace of the seventh millennium will soothe this tortured planet as restoration proceeds on schedule.

Scriptural Date of The Second Advent

Christ will not return to set his feet on the Mount of Olives on Tishri 1, the day of darkness and catastrophe. Tishri 1 is his birthday, and he will celebrate it with joy in heaven. Then he will return to walk the Earth on the following Nisan 1, on the first day of the Jewish Sacred Year, which is also their Regnal Year.

Jesus came the first time as the former rain and will return as the latter rain. As far back as Deuteronomy 11: 14, the Lord promised Israel he would send the rain of their land "in **his due season** (the Lord's due season), the first rain and the latter rain," but no one seems to have understood what he meant.

In Hosea 6:1–3, listen as the Israelites speak.

COME, and let us return unto the LORD: for he hath torn, and he will heal us; he hath smitten, and he will bind us up. After two days (two 1,000 year days) will he revive us: in the third day he will raise us up (fulfilled on time in 1948), and we shall live in his sight. Then (after 1948) shall we know, if we follow on (till 1967 when the Sign of the End of the Age appeared) to know the LORD: his going forth is prepared as the morning; and he shall come unto us as the rain, as the latter and former rain unto the earth.

God has worked a miracle for us to find in our days. The former and latter rains are such definite times in Israel that they are listed on their calendars that give the feast days and times of harvest. The former rain starts on Tishri 1, the first day of the Jewish civil year. The latter rain starts Nisan 1, the first day of their sacred and regnal year.

The month and day of the month are confirmed in Ezekiel 29:17,21. The date is set in verse 17, "in the first month, in the first day of the month." Verse 21 is the clincher.

In that day (the first month, first day, i.e., Nisan 1[12]) will I cause the horn (king, i.e., Christ)[13] of the house of Israel to bud forth.

Can you believe that the month and day of Christ's return were in the Bible all the time and we did not recognize it? Christ will take office on Earth on the same date on the Jewish calendar that all their other kings officially took office.

Since Israel will be busy for seven months burying Gog and all his multitude to "cleanse the land" (Ezekiel 39:12), there will be seven Jewish months between Christ's Coronation in heaven and his return to the Mount of Olives on Earth. This shows us that the Second Advent will take place in a Jewish leap year.

Although the Tribulation is to be shortened to 2,300 days[14], and the catastrophe will take place on Tishri 1, the last day of the 2,300, the battle of Armageddon will not start until the end of the full seven years of the Seventieth Week of Daniel. This is after Nisan 1 when Christ returns. The attack on Israel is not Armageddon because at that final battle, Christ must have already arrived on Earth.

Thy Will Be Done, on Earth, As It Is in Heaven

After he arrives, Jesus will right things on Earth and set up the Millennial government while sitting on the throne of David.

> And in mercy shall the throne be established: and he shall sit upon it in truth in the tabernacle of David, judging, and seeking judgment, and hasting righteousness.[15]

After things are straightened out here, he will return to heaven and rule everything from his throne there. King David will then sit on his own throne on Earth and be a king and prince under Christ, the King of kings and Lord of lords.

Attributes of His Throne

Heaven is a better place than Earth. Trust the Lord and make sure you make it to heaven. Descriptive words are sprinkled throughout Scripture to help us understand the supremacy of the Lord's rule, his justice and fairness, the excellent qualities of his throne, and the beauty of the place of his habitation.

> The LORD hath prepared **his throne in the heavens; and his kingdom ruleth over all** (including Earth).[16]

> **Justice and judgment** are the habitation of thy throne: **mercy and truth** shall go before thy face. Blessed is the people that know the **joyful sound:** they shall walk, O Lord, in the **light** of thy countenance.[17]

> **Honour** and **majesty** are before him: **strength** and **beauty** are in his sanctuary.[18]

Heaven's Halo

We know that His throne is in the city of New Jerusalem in the third heaven. From the various clues we have found in Scripture, it seems to me that our heaven is on the seventh planet, Saturn, the one marked off with a glorious halo of ice crystals thus look like a rainbow as they throw off sparkles in the sunlight.

The Lord probably referred to this halo as "my bow" when he set a rainbow in the clouds on Earth after Noah left the Ark. It represents his glory. The Lord told Noah,

> I do set my bow in the cloud, and it shall be for a token (*owth,* signal, beacon, or sign) of a covenant between me and the earth.[19]

Most Striking of all Planets

Saturn is swathed in beautiful thick creamy yellow-gold clouds that hide the surface, and it radiates more energy than it receives from the sun. The golden clouds furnish us a clue that the Lord is there because gold stands for deity.

In spite of being about 10 times fainter than Jupiter, Saturn is the most striking of all the planets in our solar system because of its rings. The *Backyard Astronomer's Guide* says,

> No photograph or description can adequately duplicate the astonishing beauty of the ringed planet Saturn floating against the black-velvet backdrop of the sky. Of all celestial sights available through backyard telescopes, only Saturn and the moon are sure to elicit exclamations of delight from first-time observers. Saturn casts its magic spell: beginners and veteran amateur astronomers alike never tire of the planet.[20]

I saw a photograph, made in September, 1990, showing Neptune, Uranus and Saturn. The constellation Sagittarius was in the background. In this picture, Uranus and Neptune looked no different than the background stars. They were all points of light. But, oh, how different Saturn looked. It was the brightest thing in the picture. It glowed as if on fire and seemed to reflect light on its surroundings.[21]

Heaven: A Naked-Eye Planet

There are five naked-eye planets. In order, they are Mercury, Venus, Mars, Jupiter and Saturn. Although 9.52 times as far from the sun as Earth, Saturn is huge and is easily seen in the clear sky as one of the brighter stars. It looks pearl-white or faintly cream-tinged. Since heaven is above the heads of the cherubim Mercury, Venus, and Mars, the only naked-eye planets left are Jupiter and Saturn. Only Saturn has golden clouds. Jupiter has red, orange and brown clouds.

Through a Telescope

The planet shows no crescent phase to us on the Earth, and its size varies little in a telescope.

For some unexplained reason, our view of Saturn does not seem to be affected by atmospheric turbulence as much as other celestial objects, but it still takes a telescope to view the ring structure around it. A telescope of 40 magnification can see the rings and at least Titan, the largest moon.

Titan is unusual for a satellite for two reasons. It is the second largest moon in our solar system, larger than the planet Mercury, and has a substantial nitrogen atmosphere, maybe ten times Earth's.

Although there are at least 22 and maybe as many as 30 moons orbiting around Saturn, only seven are visible in an 8'' telescope. When viewed edge-on, Saturn's rings are not visible, but the shadow they cast on the equator is often seen even then as a dark band, "the shadow of thy wings" (Psalm 17:8).

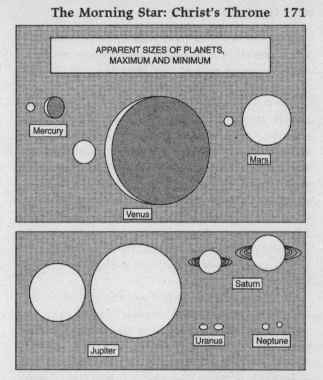

APPARENT SIZES OF PLANETS,
MAXIMUM AND MINIMUM

Mercury

Venus

Mars

Jupiter

Saturn

Uranus

Neptune

Saturn is one of the lightest planets in the solar system. It would float on water. What appears to be six rings is actually thousands of strands. The outermost one is 170,000 miles in diameter. The whole planet with its rings would span two thirds of the entire Earth-moon system.

We can't see the wealth of detail in the clouds of Saturn like on Jupiter, but there are delicate belts of different shades encircling the planet in a smooth and regular pattern. A high level haze, thought to be ammonia ice crystals, tends to subdue the contrast between features.

However, in a color photograph taken from the Voyager spacecraft, the change in color between the different bands is so distinct that there seem to be slight ridges and deeper valleys separating them.

The clouds, which have never parted to show us the surface below, are bright tawny yellow-gold in the equatorial region with what appears to be a slight ridge and then a V-shaped depression with a narrow copper line at the bottom of the V separating the equatorial area from the amber-tinged temperate zone. The temperate zone ends abruptly with a narrow belt of bright tawny yellow-gold that matches the equatorial zone. The area between that bright belt and the darker polar cap matches the temperate zone. The rings reflect tawny gold, amber, copper and cinnamon-brown in different areas.

At times a reddish or white spot can be seen, usually near the equator, but none is visible in this picture. The bands look smooth with very regular well-defined edges. To me, it looks as if the whole ball has been turned on a potter's wheel.

From Mt. Wilson's Observatory, pastel pinks, creams and yellows tinged with gold seem to tint the globe and the rings look crystalline. However you see it, the planet is strikingly beautiful. It also seems to be unique. We have not seen anything else like it out there in space.

Sometimes, Saturn almost looks like a golden eye in the sky. The ring structure flattens out to the sides and the darker polar cap surrounded with its lighter copper iris furnishes a resemblance to an eye. I can't help thinking of that when I read Psalms 17:8, ''Keep me as the apple of the eye, hide me under the shadow of thy wings.''

Wings of Silver, Feathers of Yellow Gold

After you know where it is located, certain poetical descriptions in Scripture turn out to provide pretty good visual pictures of heaven. For instance, Psalms 68:13 says,

> Though ye have lien among the pots, yet shall ye be as the wings of a dove covered with silver, and her feathers with yellow gold.

The flying heavenly body actually is covered with yellow-gold clouds and at the right inclination, the rings do look like silvery wings outspread to either side. God didn't miss a trick. He scattered clues throughout Scripture for us to find. The dove is a symbol of the Holy Spirit. That fits too.

The Morning Star

Saturn is the second largest planet in our solar system. This giant's diameter is 74,600 miles. Compare that to Earth's 7,926 miles. The orbit of Saturn is almost circular and nearly ten times the size of ours. It's distance from Earth does not change drastically. At its closest, it is 745,000,000 miles from us; at its farthest, 1,030,000,000 miles.

From that far away, the sun looks like a very brilliant blazing dot of light about one tenth the size as seen from Earth. In spite of looking like a dot, it shines with light 4,700 times as bright as our full moon.

Of the planets, Venus looks the brightest to us. It is thirteen times as bright as the star Sirius, which is the brightest star in the sky. Jupiter is next and shines 2.8 times as bright as Sirius. Saturn is half as bright as

Sirius. Mars is a little over three times the brightness of Saturn because it is closer to us.

APPARENT BRIGHTNESS

	Magnitude
Mercury	—0.2
Venus	—4.22
Mars	—2.02
Jupiter	—2.55
Saturn	—0.75

For comparison, Sirius has a magnitude of—1.42

Isaac Asimov, in his valuable reference book, *Saturn and Beyond,* said,

> Even though Jupiter is ten times as far away from Earth as Mars is, when both are at their closest Jupiter appears as the wider object. Even though Saturn is twenty-two times as far away from us as Mars is, when both are at their closest Saturn appears as an only slightly smaller object than Mars.[22]

That information could be helpful when we try to locate Saturn. Mars has a slight reddish tint that may help us see it.

Saturn has the greatest axial tilt of the naked-eye planets. Earth's axis is tipped over 23.45 degrees from the vertical. Saturn's is tipped more than Earth's, 26.73 degrees.

It moves slowly through the constellations, slower than any other naked-eye planet, partly because it is farther from the sun, partly because it moves only about one third as quickly. It is the slow planet and takes 29.5 Earth-years to orbit the sun one time.

AVERAGE ORBITAL VELOCITY

	miles per second
Mercury	29.76
Venus	21.77
Earth	18.51
Mars	14.99
Jupiter	8.52
Saturn	5.99

For five months of the year, it can be seen in the morning sky. It can also be seen in the evening sky five months. It will appear as a morning star again after March 5, 1995. Since Venus is the brightest thing in the sky after the sun and moon, it seems that a good time to find Saturn easily will come around March 13, 1995. At that time, Venus and Saturn will appear in conjunction in the morning sky.[23]

To find Saturn at other times, check *Sky & Telescope* and *Astronomy* magazines. The best time to view the outer planets is when they are crossing the meridian at midnight.

I Will Give Him The Morning Star

I believe that the Rapture, when the church will rise to meet Christ in the air and be taken to heaven, will take place on Pentecost Sunday. See *Exit: 2007, The Secret of Secrets Revealed* for details. At that time, Saturn will be a morning star. In Revelation 2:28, Jesus promised the churches,

I will give him **the morning star.** He that hath
an ear, let him hear what the Spirit saith unto
the churches.

From now through the year 2000, Saturn will be a
morning star on Pentecost. During May, 1998, Venus
will be moving toward conjunction with Saturn. As that
time approaches, it will be easy to pick out Heaven.
As a morning object, Saturn will rise before the sun
just as the church will rise before Christ returns as the
"Sun of righteousness."[24]

NIGHT SPEAKS

At that time, Saturn will be entering the constellation
Aries, the Ram. It's name comes from the Arabic word
for "The Sign," referring to alignment with the vernal
equinox early in history. The Ram suggests Christ, the
Lamb of God. Yes, "night sheweth knowledge."

THE heavens declare the glory of God; and the
firmament sheweth his handywork. Day unto day
uttereth speech, and night unto night sheweth
knowledge. There is no speech nor language,
where their voice is not heard. Their line is gone
out through all the earth, and their words to the
end of the world. In them hath he set a tabernacle
for **the sun, Which is as a bridegroom** (Christ)
coming out of his chamber.[25]

Christ Above All in World to Come

There may not be inhabitants on Uranus, Neptune
and Pluto for Ephesians 1:19–22 says that according
to the

working of his (God's) mighty power, Which he wrought in Christ, when he raised him from the dead and set him at his own right hand in the heavenly places, **Far above all principality, and power, and might, and dominion, and every name that is named,** not only in this world (*aioni,* age), but also in that which is to come (the Millennium and beyond): And hath put **all things under his feet.**

Many teach that Christ will stay on Earth for the 1,000 years that he will reign as King of kings and Lord of lords. However, the above Scripture proves otherwise. He is in the heavenly places not only in this age, but also in that which is to come.

He will come to Earth, sit on David's throne, judge the nations, set up the Millennial government, restore all things, and then go home. He will raise up king David and return him to the throne to rule as a prince under him.

The Lord's Light
There will be no night in heaven, and we will have no need of the sun. The Lord's light will be all the light we will need.

And the city (New Jerusalem) had no need of the sun, neither of the moon, to shine in it: for the glory of God did lighten it, and the Lamb (Christ) is the light thereof. And the nations of them which are saved shall walk in the light of it: and the kings of the earth do bring their glory and honour into it. And the gates of it shall not be shut at all by day: for there shall be **no night**

there. And they shall bring the glory and honour of the nations into it. And **there shall in no wise enter into it any thing that defileth,** neither whatsoever worketh abomination, or maketh a lie: but they which are written in the Lamb's book of life.

Jesus said, "I am the light of the world,"[26] and let his light shine forth at the Transfiguration to give us an example of his glory.

AND after six days (prefiguring the Rapture in the 6,000th year since man became mortal when Adam left Eden) Jesus taketh Peter, James, and John his brother, and **bringeth them up** into an high mountain apart (symbolizing heaven). And was transfigured before them: and his face did shine **as the sun,** and his raiment was white as the light.[27]

Saturday Sabbath

Saturday, Saturn's day, is the Jewish Sabbath. I believe Jesus was born on the Feast of Trumpets on September 8, B.C. 5. It was the Saturday Sabbath. He is Lord of the Sabbath—Saturday—Saturn. It all ties together. He said that "the Son of man is Lord also of the sabbath."[28]

Christ: Lord of Heaven and Earth

Know therefore this day, and consider it in thine heart, that the LORD he is God in heaven above, and upon the earth beneath: there is none else.[29]

God that made the world and all things therein . . . he is Lord of heaven and earth.[30]

Three Are One

For there are three that bear record in heaven, the Father, the Word (Jesus Christ[31]), and the Holy Ghost: and these three are one.[32]

As The Angels

There will be angels in heaven and no marriage. Mark 12:25 says that we will be as the angels:

For when they shall rise from the dead, they neither marry, nor are given in marriage; but are **as the angels** which are in heaven.

Overcomers Leap for Joy

The beatitudes give us insight into what heaven will be like. God is fair. He will reward us for trusting him, for putting up with things that hit us hard, for taking just one step at a time and not getting discouraged, and for being overcomers to the end.

Luke 6:20–23,35–38 is a wonderful passage to read when you feel like there is no justice and this world stinks. Thank God there is a flip side to that coin. Jesus promised,

Blessed be ye poor: for your's in the kingdom of God. Blessed are ye that hunger now: for **ye shall be filled.** Blessed are ye that weep now: for **ye**

shall laugh. Blessed are ye, when men shall hate you, and when they shall separate you from their company, and shall reproach you, and cast out your name as evil, for the Son of man's sake. Rejoice ye in that day, and **leap for joy:** for, behold, **your reward is great in heaven:** for in the like manner did their fathers unto the prophets. . . . But love ye your enemies, and do good, and lend, hoping for nothing again; and your reward shall be great, and **ye shall be the children of the Highest** . . . forgive, and ye shall be **forgiven:** Give, and **it shall be given unto you; good measure,** pressed down, and shaken together, and running over, shall men give into your bosom. For **with the same measure that ye mete withal it shall be measured to you again.**

An Enduring Substance

Heaven is a better country.[33] Moths and rust do not corrupt. Thieves do not break through and steal. Just to be with Christ is far better. Scripture says,

Ye have in heaven **a better and an enduring substance.**[34]

I (Paul) am in a strait betwixt two, having a desire to depart, and to be with Christ; which is **far better:** Nevertheless to abide in the flesh is more needful for you.[35]

But lay up for yourselves treasures in heaven, where **neither moth nor rust doth corrupt,** and where **thieves do not break through nor steal:**

For where your treasure is, there will your heart
be also.[36]

Blessed be the God and Father of our Lord Jesus
Christ, which according to his abundant mercy
hath begotten us again unto a lively hope by the
resurrection of Jesus Christ from the dead, To **an
inheritance incorruptible, and undefiled,** and
that fadeth not away, reserved in heaven for
you.[37]

Day of Rewards, Good and Bad

We will receive our rewards in heaven right after
Rapture II snatches the Tribulation saints out of the
fire. This will take place on the same day but before
the asteroid strikes Earth. The asteroid impact is the
reward for unbelief. The saints are promised, "Only
with thine eyes shalt thou behold and see the reward
of the wicked."[38]

The Judgment Seat of Christ takes place after Christ
is crowned in heaven but before he returns to place his
feet on the Mount of Olives.

But the LORD shall endure for ever: **he hath
prepared his throne for judgment.** And he shall
judge the world in righteousness.[39]

Daniel described the scene in heaven when Christ is
given dominion. After the thrones were placed,

the Ancient of days did sit, whose garment was
white as snow, and the hair of his head like the

pure wool: **his throne was like the fiery flame, and his wheels as burning fire.**

The throne like the fiery flame is similar to Ezekiel 1:13, where the cherubim are said to have the appearance of burning coals of fire. The word translated "wheels" is *galgal,* whirling things. It represents the orbit, which looked like burning fire as it reflected the fiery-looking globe.

Continuing, Daniel said,

one like the Son of man (Jesus Christ) came with the clouds of heaven (Saturn's golden clouds), and came to the Ancient of days . . . And **there was given him dominion, and glory, and a kingdom,** that all people, nations, and languages, should serve him.[40]

In Revelation 11, John showed us that God's wrath will take place at the same time the saints are rewarded in heaven. It will follow the coronation ceremony on what the Old Testament calls "that day," the Feast of Trumpets that begins the Millennium. Note in the following Scripture that on the Day of God's Wrath, the Second Advent is still future.

We give thee thanks, O Lord God Almighty (Jesus Christ), which art, and wast, and **art to come;** because thou hast taken to thee thy great power, and hast **reigned.** And the nations were angry, and **thy wrath is come,** and the time of the dead, that they should be judged, **and that thou shouldest give reward unto thy servants** the prophets, and to the saints . . . **and shouldest**

destroy them which destroy the earth. And the temple of God was opened in heaven, and there was seen in his temple the ark of his testament: and there were lightnings, and voices, and thunderings, and an earthquake, and great hail.[41]

Rapture II: The First Sharp Sickle

Before the asteroid (little star) impacts Earth, Rapture II must take place. It also takes place on "that day." John saw a vision of it happening after Christ receives his golden crown and before his wrath is poured out. He said,

> I looked, and behold a white cloud, and upon the cloud one sat like unto the Son of man (Jesus Christ), having **on his head a golden crown, and in his hand a sharp sickle.** And another angel came out of the temple, crying with a loud voice to him that sat on the cloud, Thrust in thy sickle, and reap . . . for **the harvest of the earth** is ripe. And he that sat on the cloud thrust in his sickle on the earth; and **the earth was reaped.**[42]

The word translated "sickle" is *drepanon*, a gathering hook, from *drepo*, to pluck. This is when Christ gathers the rest of the Christians and takes them to heaven to participate in the Award Ceremony. They come out of all nations and include the Laodiceans. The people who saw the first Rapture and believed plus all who accept Christ during the Tribulation are also included. John described this. He said,

> I beheld, and, lo, a great multitude, which no man could number, of all nations . . . stood before the

throne . . . **These are they which came out of great tribulation,** and have washed their robes, and made them white in the blood of the Lamb. Therefore are they before the throne . . . They shall **hunger no more, neither thirst** any more; neither shall the sun light on them (because of Saturn's thick clouds), nor any heat (*kauma,* consuming heat) . . . and **God shall wipe away all tears** from their eyes.[43]

"The LORD preserveth all them that love him (Raptures I and II): but all the wicked will he destroy" on the same day that Rapture II takes place.[44] After the Tribulation saints are safely out of the way, the fire will fall. Thus, they will literally be "saved; yet so as by fire."[45] This is similar to the time Lot and his daughters barely made it out of Sodom before the cities of the plains were destroyed by fire and brimstone.[46] As soon as the Tribulation saints join the Old Testament and Church saints in heaven, they stand before the Judgment Seat of Christ.

The Bema Seat

The judgment seat of Christ is called the Bema Seat from the Greek word *bema* used in II Corinthians 5:10 and Romans 14:10,11, which says,

But why dost thou judge thy brother: or why dost thou set at nought thy brother? for we shall all stand before the judgment seat (*bemati*) of Christ. For it is written (in Isaiah 45:23), As I live, saith the Lord, every knee shall bow to me, and every tongue shall confess to God.

For we must all appear before the judgment seat (*bematos*) of Christ; that every one may receive the things done in his body, according to that he hath done, whether it be good or bad.

Judgment of believer's works, not sins, is in view here. By this time, we are in heaven; we have already received that reward. The sins have been paid for by Christ himself, and we have already been saved.

The result of this judgment of our works is like the two sides of a flash card. One side says RECEIVE REWARDS, he flip side, LOSE REWARDS.

Which will it be for you? RECEIVE or LOSE? RECEIVE or LOSE?

Remember, we only have this one lifetime on Earth to earn these precious rewards. There is no reincarnation, no coming back to try it again. The Lord has decreed that the just must walk by faith.[47] That is our test. If we were to come back, the test could no longer be by walking by faith. We would know too much.

And as it is appointed unto men **once to die, but after this the judgment:** So Christ was once offered to bear the sins of many; and unto them that look for him shall he appear the second time without sin unto salvation.[48]

Are you looking for him? He told us about 23 times to watch. If we watch, we will be looking for him for we will **know** when he is coming for us at the Rapture. Jesus warned,

If therefore thou shalt not watch, I will come on
thee as a thief, and thou shalt not know what hour
I will come upon thee.

Jesus knew that if we watched, we would first be
able to recognize the Sign of the End of the Age—the
Six-Day War of 1967 when Israel grew leaves[49]—and
at that time, also be able to figure out exactly when the
Rapture would take place. (See my book *Exit: 2007,
The Secret of Secrets Revealed,* for all the details on
how to make the calculations.)

In 30 A.D., no man knew the day or hour. Since the
Sign of the End of the Age pegged God's Blueprint of
Time to our calendar, we can know when he will come
to take us to heaven.

We are privileged people. We know the Rapture is
nigh. We live in the time of the end when knowledge
is increased. This knowledge offsets the constantly
worsening conditions we have to live under because of
the approaching Tribulation. We can patiently put up
with whatever is required because we know our trip to
heaven is coming up soon. Keep your eyes on Him and
walk one step at a time. We are almost home. Be an
overcomer. Secure those precious rewards that are now
drawing near, "for the time is at hand."[50] Jesus
promised,

Because thou hast kept the word of my patience,
I also will keep thee from the hour of temptation
(the Tribulation), which shall come upon all the
world, to try them that dwell upon the earth. Behold, I come quickly: hold that fast which thou
hast, that no man take thy crown. Him that over-

cometh will I make a pillar in the temple of my
God, and he shall go no more out: and I will
write upon him the name of my God, and the
name of the city of my God, which is New
Jerusalem.[51]

Another Sharp Sickle

As John tells us of his vision of the second sharp
sickle, you can see that there is a connection between
the brazen altar and the Earth. This second sharp sickle
is the flaming sword that was placed to the East of
Eden in Genesis 3:24.

And **another angel came out of the temple**
which is in heaven, he also having a sharp
sickle. And **another angel came out from the
altar** (representing Earth), which had power
over fire; and cried with a loud cry . . . Thrust
in thy sharp sickle, and gather the clusters of
the vine **of the earth;** for her **grapes are fully
ripe** (it is **the vintage**—September—the Feast
of Trumpets). And the angel thrust in his sickle
into the earth, and gathered the vine **of the
earth,** and **cast it into the great winepress of
the wrath of God.**[52]

No More Ark

This is when the stone tablet in the Ark is dumped
out and the burnt offering is offered up on the altar of
Earth. The Ark is not mentioned again. It's purpose has
been fulfilled. Scripture says,

A wise **king** (the King of kings) scattereth the wicked, and bringeth the **wheel** (*owphan,* revolve, orbit of the asteroid) over them.[53]

And it shall come to pass, when ye be multiplied and increased in the land, in those days (after Christ's return), saith the LORD, they shall say no more, The ark of the covenant of the LORD: neither shall it come to mind: neither shall they remember it; neither shall they visit it; neither shall that be done any more.[54]

When men try try their hand at keeping the asteroid from being dumped on Earth, it won't work. The wrath of God will be poured out; Earth will be threshed.

This was dramatized for us in I Chronicles 13:9,10. Uzza put forth his hand to keep the Ark and the stones within it from being dumped on the ground and was struck dead in the Lord's anger.

And when they came unto the threshingfloor of Chidon, Uzza put forth his hand to hold the ark; for the oxen stumbled. And the anger of the LORD was kindled against Uzza, and he smote him, because he put his hand to the ark:[55] and there he died before God.

This coming judgment will not be stopped. The stone will strike the Earth on the Day of God's Wrath.

The Seven Month Gap

After Christ is crowned in heaven, the catastrophic judgment precedes his return to Earth. He could not return in glory in the midst of such a great disaster, so he shows them the Sign of the Son of Man and only makes his presence felt.

Seven Jewish months later, he actually sets his feet on the Mount of Olives. Scripture shows that the catastrophic fire precedes his return.

> The LORD is in his holy temple, the LORD'S throne is **in heaven** . . . Upon the wicked he shall rain **snares, fire** and **brimstone,** and an **horrible tempest:** this shall be the portion of their cup.[56]

> **THE LORD reigneth** . . . righteousness and judgment are the habitation of his throne. **A fire goeth before him,** and burneth up his enemies round about. His lightnings enlightened the world: the earth saw, and trembled. The hills melted like wax at the presence of the LORD, at the presence of the Lord of the whole earth. The heavens declare his righteousness (the Sign of the Son of Man is seen in heaven[57]), and all the people see his glory.[58]

The land of Israel must be cleansed before Christ can actually return in glory. In chapter 39, Ezekiel explained what happens in Israel during that seven month interval.

> And **seven months** shall the house of Israel be burying of them, that they may **cleanse the land.** Yea, all the people of the land shall bury them; and it shall be to them a renown **the day that I shall be glorified** (the day of the Second Advent), saith the Lord GOD.[59]

The Attack on Israel Provokes God's Fury

What brings on the catastrophe is the multinational attack on Israel. Gog means roof, covering, i.e., top. He is the top leader of the army that aims to wipe Israel off the map. The Lord God said,

> And it shall come to pass **at the same time when Gog shall come against the land of Israel** . . . that **my fury shall come up in my face**. . . . in that day there shall be a great shaking . . . **and all the men that are upon the face of the earth, shall shake** at my presence, and the mountains shall be thrown down . . . and every wall shall fall . . . I will rain upon him, and upon his bands, and upon the many people that are with him, an overflowing rain (shower, i.e., a tidal wave), and great **hailstones, fire,** and **brimstone.** Thus will I magnify myself, and sanctify myself: and I will be known (seen) in the eyes of many nations (the Sign of the Son of Man), and they shall know that I am the LORD.[60]

Saints Judge Israel, World, and Angels

After Rapture II, Christ will sit as judge at the Judgment Seat of Christ. He will delegate duties to his saints. They will also judge. They are to judge Israel, the world, and the angels.

(1) Israel

> Jesus said unto them, Verily I say unto you, That ye which have followed me, in the regeneration when the Son of man shall sit in the throne of

his glory, ye also shall sit upon twelve thrones, **judging the twelve tribes of Israel.** And every one that hath forsaken houses, or brethren, or sisters, or father, or mother, or wife, or children, or lands, for my name's sake, shall receive an hundredfold, and shall inherit everlasting life (Matt. 19:28,29).

Ye are they which have continued with me in my temptations. And I appoint unto you a kingdom, as my Father hath appointed unto me; That ye may eat and drink at my table in my kingdom, and sit on thrones **judging the twelve tribes of Israel** (Luke 22:28–30).

(2) The world

Do ye not know that **the saints shall judge the world?** and if the world shall be judged by you, are ye unworthy to judge the smallest matters? (I Corinthians 6:2).

PRAISE ye the LORD. Sing unto the LORD a new song (after the Rapture)[61], and his praise in the congregation of saints (in heaven[62]). . . . Let the saints be joyful in glory: let them sing aloud upon their beds. Let the high praises of God be in their mouth, and a **twoedged sword in their hand;** To execute vengeance upon the heathen, and punishments upon the people; To bind their kings with chains, and their nobles with fetters of iron; **To execute upon them the judgment written: this honour have all his saints.**[63]

(3) Angels

Know ye not that **we shall judge angels?**[64]

The Angels of the Seven Churches

In Revelation 1:20, Jesus said, "The seven stars are the angels of the seven churches." Since the saints shall judge the world and execute the judgment written, the seven angels that are given seven trumpets that bring judgment are probably the angels of the seven churches. Revelation 8:2 says,

> And I saw the (*tous,* the) seven angels which stood before God; and to them were given seven trumpets.

When the article "the" is given, it usually refers to something that we have already been introduced to. Therefore, we should be able to figure out who these angels are, and we have already been introduced to the seven angels of the seven churches. We are to be as the angels after the Resurrection.

When we first saw the seven angels, they were in Christ's hand because he had just plucked them up at the Rapture. By the second Rapture, "all the angels stood round about the throne . . . and fell before the throne on their faces, and worshipped God."[65] Thus, the seven angels of the churches are there before God when the seven trumpets are given out.

The Golden Censer

As the next verse begins, we see "another" angel introduced. The globe shaped golden censer representing the asteroid is given to him to cast to the Earth. The seven trumpet judgments show the immediate effect of the impact. The seven vials reflect the ultimate effect.

The Branch

Israel is the branch of the fig tree. Jesus is the branch of God. He will not only be the King of kings, but he will also be the Lord of lords. He will be a priest upon the throne (something the Satan-possessed False Prophet will copy in his attempt to be like the Most High).

> The BRANCH . . . he shall build the temple of the LORD: and he shall bear the glory, and shall sit and rule upon his throne; and **he shall be a priest upon his throne:** and the counsel of peace shall be between them both.[66]

The Live Coal

Isaiah had a very symbolic experience with one of the seraphim. He said,

> I saw also the Lord sitting upon a throne, high and lifted up . . . Woe is me! for I am undone; because I am a man of unclean lips, and I dwell in the midst of a people of unclean lips: for mine eyes have seen the King, the LORD of hosts. **Then flew one of the seraphims unto me, having a live coal in his hand,** which he had taken with the tongs from off the altar: And he laid it upon my mouth, and said, Lo, this hath touched

thy lips; and thine iniquity is taken away, and thy sin purged.[67]

The live coal is a type of the asteroid that will purge the Earth of wickedness. Don't be here on that dreadful day. Take the free ticket to heaven that Christ bought for you. Accept Jesus as your own personal Saviour. Go in the Rapture.

✠ *Notes*

CHAPTER 1: HEAVEN: REAL AND VISIBLE

[1] John 14:2
[2] Revelation 1:3
[3] Daniel 12:4,9
[4] Psalms 96:5,6
[5] Psalms 24:10
[6] Revelation 22:3
[7] II Chronicles 2:6
[8] Nehemiah 9:6
[9] Isaiah 66:1
[10] Psalms 115:16
[11] Revelation 2:7
[12] Revelation 21:10; 22:2
[13] Matthew 22:32
[14] Revelation 3:12
[15] Revelation 21:14

[16] Hebrews 11:10,13–16
[17] John 14:2
[18] Revelation 21:16,18;22:3,4
[19] Hebrews 6:20
[20] Unger's Bible Dictionary, p. 658
[21] Revelation 21:16
[22] Genesis 3:24; Ezekiel 1 and 10
[23] Genesis 3:24
[24] Revelation 22:3
[25] Hebrews 8:1,2,5
[26] Isaiah 40:22
[27] Psalms 99:1
[28] I Chronicles 13:6 RSV
[29] Revelation 22:3
[30] Strong's concordance
[31] Mark 13:23
[32] Isaiah 28:9–13
[33] Romans 10:9
[34] It has golden clouds and is in the third heaven.

CHAPTER 2: CHARIOT OF THE CHERUBIM

[1] Ezekiel 34:24
[2] Jeremiah 30:9
[3] Ezekiel 37:25
[4] Bible Institute of Los Angeles
[5] Ezekiel 1:5
[6] "to," as in the NIV, NASB, NEB and JB
[7] Genesis 3:24
[8] Revelation 21:27
[9] Ezekiel 39:12
[10] Genesis 3:17
[11] Halley's Bible Handbook, p. 27

[12] I Chronicles 28:18
[13] Leviticus 26:23–25
[14] Psalms 104:30
[15] Galatians 3:28
[16] Numbers 14:14
[17] Psalms 102:25
[18] Psalms 8:3,4
[19] Revelation 12:9
[20] Robbins, Gary. "Cosmic Rain," *The Orange County Register,* August 4, 1994
[21] Popular Science, July, 1994, p. 45.
[22] Matthew 24:22
[23] Mullen, William. "Stardust," *The Orange County Register,* June 28, 1994
[24] Psalms 78:69
[25] Revelation 21:1
[26] Isaiah 24:1–6
[27] Psalm 75:3 NIV
[28] Revelation 17:15
[29] Joshua 6:25
[30] Job 26:12 NASB
[31] Psalms 89:10
[32] Isaiah 53:1,5
[33] Isaiah 51:9
[34] Gesenius' Hebrew-Chaldee Lexicon of the Old Testament, pg. 761
[35] Gesenius. Ibid, pg. 503
[36] Exodus 26:1
[37] Exodus 26:6
[38] II Kings 19:15
[39] Jeremiah 50:23
[40] Ezekiel 39:12,13
[41] Daniel 2:34,35,44,45
[42] Jeremiah 50:25

[43] Jeremiah 46:10
[44] Joshua 10:11–13
[45] Ezekiel 1:8
[46] I Kings 8:8[47] Ibid.
[48] Matthew 24:33
[49] I Corinthians 3:15
[50] Zechariah 5:11
[51] Revelation 13:7,8
[52] Hebrews 5:14
[53] Luke 21:24
[54] Ezekiel 38:18–23
[55] Romans 3:23–25, Green's Interlinear
[56] 1 John 2:2

CHAPTER 3: THE VENGEANCE OF HIS TEMPLE

[1] Revelation 6:10
[2] Revelation 8:3
[3] Jeremiah 51:6–9
[4] Dyer, Charles H. *The Rise of Babylon.* (Wheaton, IL: Tyndale House Publishers, 1991)
[5] Revelation 18:4,5,8
[6] Jeremiah 51:49
[7] Revelation 18:9,10
[8] Jeremiah 26:33
[9] Ezekiel 38:20
[10] Revelation 16:18–21
[11] Isaiah 27:12
[12] Ezekiel 29:12
[13] Unger's Bible Dictionary, p. 257
[14] Daniel 3:26–28
[15] I Corinthians 3:11–15
[16] Jeremiah 51:25

[17] Isaiah 52:10; 53:1
[18] Jeremiah 12:12
[19] Zechariah 11:17
[20] Revelation 8:11
[21] Ezekiel 10:2,6
[22] Matthew 24:22
[23] Revelation 8:8,10
[24] Ezekiel 39:2–4
[25] Ezekiel 47:18
[26] Deuteronomy 11:24; 34:2
[27] Joel 2:20
[28] Ezekiel 39:15,16
[29] Ezekiel 39:12
[30] Joel 2:2; Zephaniah 1:15
[31] Jeremiah 3:16,17
[32] ''Cosmic Rain,'' *The Orange County Register.* Aug. 4, 1994, page 12
[33] Ezekiel 29:8–11
[34] Jeremiah 25:31
[35] Ephesians 2:8–10
[36] Romans 10:8–10
[37] John 2:1,2

CHAPTER 4: THE SECRET OF HIS TABERNACLE

[1] Jeremiah 30:7
[2] Psalms 27:4
[3] Daniel 8:13,14
[4] Joel 1:15
[5] Malachi 2:2,3; Hosea 9:5–7; Joel 2:1–20
[6] Nahum 2:3
[7] Revelation 1:8
[8] Psalms 91:1–9

9   Exodus 24:10

10 Ezekiel 10:1

11 Ezekiel 10:19–21

12 Webster's Seventh New Collegiate Dictionary, p. 763

13 Exodus 24:10

14 Hebrews 11:16

15 Job 1:6,7

16 Ezekiel 28:14–18

17 Genesis 3:24

18 Revelation 22:1

19 Amos 8:9,10

20 Job 21:23–29

21 Malachi 2:1–3

22 Hosea 9:5–7

23 Joel 2:1,2

24 Zephaniah 1:15,16

25 "Cosmic Rain," *The Orange County Register,* Aug. 4, 1994, NEWS, p. 12.

26 Jeremiah 52:12; Josephus. Wars of the Jews. Book 6, Ch. 4, sect. 5

27 "Tisha Be'Av -vs- Jupiter!!??." text file JUPITE. TXT, posted on CompuServe by James MacLean, CS ID #73554,1160 with permission. Originally Article #41307, from bmirabito @aol.com (BMirabito)

28 Ezekiel 21:9–14

29 Josephus. Wars of the Jews, Book 4, Ch. 8, sect. 4.

30 Sellier, Charles E. and Russell, Brian. Ancient Secrets of the Bible. (N.Y.: Dell Publishing, 1994) pp. 53,71,87

31 Revelation 13:8,12

32 Revelation 13:7,12

33 Ezekiel 39:12

34 Ezekiel 21:15–27

35 Revelation 13:8

36 Revelation 13:7
37 Revelation 13:5
38 Revelation 14:20
39 Isaiah 34:8–10
40 Zechariah 5:11
41 Colossians 1:19
42 Colossians 1:15
43 Green's Interlinear
44 Psalms 104:1–3
45 Psalms 19:6
46 II Corinthians 12:2
47 Psalms 89:36,37
48 Revelation 2:28,29
49 Matthew 2:2
50 Matthew 24:27
51 Ezekiel 1:22, NWT
52 Gesenius' Lexicon
53 Ezekiel 1:13
54 Matthew 6:10
55 I Samuel 17:50
56 Revelation 8:11
57 Revelation 3:10
58 Revelation 5:9
59 I Corinthians 3:15
60 Jeremiah 30:7
61 II Samuel 22:5–20
62 Psalms 27:5
63 Revelation 7:14–17
64 Acts 5:1–10
65 Colossians 2:9
66 John 1:3
67 John 4:24
68 Acts 17:28
69 Deuteronomy 10:14

70 John 1:18
71 Revelation 22:3–5
72 Matthew 13:45,46
73 Ezekiel 1:26–28
74 Habakkuk 3:3
75 Hebrews 8:2
76 John 14:3
77 Hebrews 7:3

CHAPTER 5: THE TABERNACLE PATTERN

1   Exodus 25:22
2   Berakot 8b; Baba Bathra 14b; as stated by Price, Randall. (Eugene Oregon: Harvest House Publishers, 1994) pp. 137, 366.
3   Isaiah 66:1
4   Revelation 22:3
5   Isaiah 9:7
6   Jeremiah 30:9
7   Ezekiel 34:24
8   Exodus 20:24
9   Ezekiel 29:10,11
10 Revelation 18:9.
11 Ezekiel 21:15
12 Exodus 29:38,39
13 I Corinthians 5:7
14 Hebrews 9:26
15 Zephaniah 1:7,8,10,15
16 Revelation 9:1,2
17 John 6:33,35
18 Hebrews 10:20
19 Hebrews 9:22
20 Exodus 30:10
21 Romans 12:19

22 Revelation 18:6
23 Jeremiah 17:17,18
24 Revelation 8:4,5
25 Isaiah 24:1
26 Ezekiel 38:20
27 Psalms 99:1
28 Psalms 78:25
29 Zechariah 5:4
30 Isaiah 40:22
31 Exodus 30:8
32 Exodus 20:4
33 Revelation 18:4
34 Genesis 3:17
35 Jeremiah 46:10
36 Colossians 2:2,3
37 John 8:23-28
38 I John 5:11-20
39 I Thessalonians 4:14,17
40 Romans 10:9
41 II Corinthians 5:19
42 Acts 4:12
43 Isaiah 44:6
44 Revelation 1:5,8
45 Revelation 22:12-14
46 Revelation 21:21
47 Hebrews 5:5-14

CHAPTER 6: THE MORNING STAR: CHRIST'S THRONE

1 Jeremiah 30:7
2 Revelation 18:12,16
3 John 5:22
4 Matthew 24:30

[5] Luke 12:35–37
[6] John 3:29
[7] Revelation 11:15–19
[8] Ezekiel 39:12,13
[9] Matthew 25:41
[10] Revelation 19:17–21
[11] Revelation 20:2
[12] Ezekiel 45:18
[13] Psalms 132:17; Luke 1:69
[14] Daniel 8:14
[15] Isaiah 16:5
[16] Psalms 103:19
[17] Psalms 89:14,15
[18] Psalms 96:6
[19] Genesis 9:13
[20] Dickinson, Terence and Dyer, Alan. *The Backyard Astronomer's Guide.* (Camden East, Ontario, Canada, Camden House, 1991) p. 154.
[21] Ibid, p. 144.
[22] Asimov, Isaac. *Saturn and Beyond.* (NY: Lothrop, Lee & Shepard Co., 1979) p. 46.
[23] Whitney, Charles A. *Whitney's Star Finder.* (N.Y.: Alfred A. Knopf, 1989) p. 100.
[24] Malachi 4:2
[25] Psalms 19:1–5
[26] John 8:12
[27] Matthew 17:1,2
[28] Luke 6:5
[29] Deuteronomy 4:39
[30] Acts 7:24
[31] Revelation 19:13
[32] I John 5:7
[33] Hebrews 11:16
[34] Hebrews 10:34

[35] Philippians 1:23,24
[36] Matthew 6:20,21
[37] I Peter 1:3,4
[38] Psalms 91:8
[39] Psalms 9:7,8
[40] Daniel 7:9,13,14
[41] Revelation 11:17–19
[42] Revelation 14:14–16
[43] Revelation 7:9–17
[44] Psalms 145:20
[45] I Corinthians 3:15
[46] Luke 17:29
[47] II Corinthians 5:7
[48] Hebrews 9:27,28
[49] Matthew 24:32
[50] Revelation 1:3
[51] Revelation 3:10–12
[52] Revelation 14:16–19
[53] Proverbs 20:26
[54] Jeremiah 3:16
[55] See Numbers 4:15
[56] Psalms 11:4,6
[57] Matthew 24:30
[58] Psalms 97:1–6
[59] Ezekiel 39:12,13
[60] Ezekiel 38:18–23
[61] Revelation 5:9
[62] Hebrews 12:22,23
[63] Psalms 149:1,5–9
[64] I Corinthians 6:3
[65] Revelation 7:11
[66] Zechariah 6:12,13
[67] Isaiah 6:1–8

✢ Selected Bibliography

Agee, M.J. *Exit: 2007, The Secret of Secrets Revealed.* (Yorba Linda, CA.: Archer Press, 1991)

The Amplified New Testament. (Grand Rapids: Zondervan Publishing House, 1968)

The Amplified Old Testament. (Grand Rapids: Zondervan Publishing House, 1962)

Asimov, Isaac. *Saturn and Beyond.* (NY: Lothrop, Lee & Shepard Co., 1979)

The Bible, Revised Standard Version. (NY: American Bible Society, 1952)

Brenton, Sir Lancelot C.L. *The Septuagint Version: Greek and English* (Grand Rapids: Zondervan Publishing House, originally published by Samuel Bagster & Sons, London, 1851)

Chapman, Clark R. *Planets of Rock and Ice.* (NY: Charles Scribner's Sons, 1982)

206

Concordant Literal New Testament. (Canyon Country, CA.: Concordant Publishing Concern, 1983)

Concordant Versions of Genesis, Exodus, Deuteronomy, Leviticus and Numbers, Isaiah, Ezekiel, and The Minor Prophets. (Canyon Country, CA.: Concordant Publishing Concern, different dates for each)

Cornell, James and Gorenstein, Paul, ed. *Astronomy from Space.* (Cambridge, MA: The MIT Press, 1983)

Dunlop, Storm, ed. *Atlas of the Night Sky.* (NY: Crescent Books, 1984)

Dyer, Charles H. *The Rise of Babylon.* (Wheaton, IL: Tyndale House Publishers, 1991)

French, Bevan M. and Maran, Stephen P., ed: *A Meeting with the Universe; Science Discoveries from the Space Program.* (Washington, D.C.: National Aeronautics and Space Administration, 1981)

Tregelles, Samuel Prideaux, translator, *Gesenius' Hebrew and Chaldee Lexicon.* (Grand Rapids: Baker Book House, 1979)

Goldsmith, Donald. *The Evolving Universe.* (Menlo Park, (CA: Benjamin Cuimmings Publishing Co, Inc., 1981)

Green, Jay. *The Interlinear Hebrew/Greek-English Bible.* (Wilmington, DE: Associated Publishers and Authors, 1976)

Halley, Henry H. *Halley's Bible Handbook.* (Minneapolis, MN: Zondervan Publishing House, 1962)

Harrington, Phillip S. *Touring the Universe Through Binoculars.* (NY: John Wiley and Sons, 1990)

Holy Bible, The Berkeley Version. (Grand Rapids: Zondervan Publishing House, 1959)

The Holy Bible, King James Version. (Nashville: Thomas Nelson Publishers, 1977)

The Holy Bible, New American Catholic Edition. (NY: Benziger Brothers, Inc., 1952)

The Holy Bible, New International Version. (East Brunswick, NJ: International Bible Society, 1984)

The Holy Bible. The Scofield Reference Bible. (NY: Oxford University Press, 1917)

Lamsa, George M. *The Holy Bible from Ancient Eastern Manuscripts.* (Philadelphia: A.J. Holman Co., 1957)

Mullen, William. "Stardust," *The Orange County Register,* June 28, 1994

The New American Bible. Catholic Biblical Association of America. (NY: World Publishing, 1970)

New American Standard Bible. (NY: Thomas Nelson, Publishers, 1977)

The New Jerusalem Bible. (NY: Doubleday, 1990)

Peterson, Roger Tory. *Stars and Planets.* (Norwalk, CT: Easton Press, 1983)

Preiss, Byron, ed. *The Planets.* (NY: Bantam Books, 1985)

Price, Randall. *In Search of Temple Treasures.* (Eugene, Oregon: Harvest House Publishers, 1994)

Robbins, Gary, "Cosmic Rain," *The Orange County Register,* August 4, 199???

Saint Joseph Edition of the Holy Bible. NY: Catholic Book Publishing Co., 1963)

Sellier, Charles E. and Russell, Brian. *Ancient Secrets of the Bible.* (NY: Dell Publishing, 1994)

Strong, James. *The Exhaustive Concordance of the Bible.* (NY: Abingdon Press, 1967)

Thayer, Joseph Henry. *Thayer's Greek-English Lexicon*

of the New Testament. (Grand Rapids: Associated Publishers and Authors, Inc., nd)

Unger, Merrill F. *Unger's Bible Dictionary.* (Chicago: Moody Press, 1969)

Young, Robert. *Young's Analytical Concordance.* (Grand Rapids: Associated Publishers and Authors, Inc., nd)

✢ Index

Altar of earth, 142
Altar of Incense, 148
Ark, 58, 84, 87, 140, 151,
    169, 183, 188
Armageddon, 35, 112, 165,
    167
Ash layer, 111
Ash-colored horses, 129
Asteroid, 53, 65, 72, 78, 80,
    81, 87, 94, 103, 104,
    149, 150, 181, 188,
    193, 194
Asteroid Belt, 49, 50, 51,
    52, 101, 140
Asteroid impact, 38, 87, 88,
    103, 113, 181
Astronomers, 107, 109

Babylon, 69, 70, 71, 79, 84,
    90, 95, 104, 110, 113,
    143, 149

Babylon International Festi-
    val, 69
"Be still and know that I
    am God.", 31
Beast, 46, 112, 114, 165
Beginning of revenges, 35
Bema Seat, 184
Between the cherubim, 50,
    81
Birthday of Jesus, 164, 165
Blueprint of Time, 186
Brazen Altar, 143
Brazen mountains, 130
Bride of Christ, 164

Catastrophe, 165
Celestial map, 127, 141
Censer, 150, 151, 192
Chariot of fire, 64

Chariot of the cherubim, 25, 36, 58, 66, 84, 92

Cherub, 80, 81, 101, 101

Cherubim, 15, 18, 20, 23, 25, 26, 27, 30, 42, 47, 50, 51, 52, 55, 57, 58, 66, 81, 96, 97, 107, 128, 140, 148, 151, 153, 182

Chicxulub Crater, 43, 88

Chiun, 152

Circuit of heaven, 122

Clues, 22, 67

Coals of fire, 25, 50, 52, 55, 65, 80, 81, 116

Collision, 81, 90, 108, 109

Commandments, ten, 73

Corner, 129

Coronation ceremony, 162, 182

Creation week, 38

Crown, 112

Crucifixion, 105

Curse, 30, 78, 113, 140, 145, 147, 155

Curtain, 18, 48, 67, 119, 120, 121, 128, 152, 153, 154

David, 24, 130, 142

Day of Atonement, 106
of darkness, 107
of destruction, 85, 106, 164
of God's Wrath, 83, 104, 164, 188
of preparation, 82, 93, 105
of the Lord, 93, 164
of vengeance, 53, 155

Days of Awe, 105
of recompence, 85

Dead Sea, 84

Device, 54, 69, 90

Diameter, 141, 171, 173

Dominion, 162, 181

Doomsday rock, 51

Doors, 60

Double destruction, 149

Earthquake, 72, 150, 183

East of Eden, 33, 125

Egypt, 82, 85, 88

Eleanor Helin, 87, 108

Emerald, 103, 114, 115

Equator, 136

Eridu, 36

Esther, 164

Euphrates River, 73, 82

False Prophet, 46, 79, 81, 104, 107, 112, 129, 165, 193

Father, the everlasting, 8

Feast of Trumpets, 77, 82, 84, 85, 93, 107, 129, 145, 162, 163, 164, 182

Feast of Weeks, 62

First and last, 8, 114

Firstfruits, 105

Flaming sword, 32, 33, 34, 35, 36, 46, 53, 64, 66, 78, 79, 83, 94, 107, 110, 187

Footstool, 142

Former and latter rain, 166
Forty years, 73, 89
Four chariots, 130
Foursquare, 4, 13

Giant planet, 97, 121
Glittering sword, 35
Glory, 169
Goats, 164
God was in Christ, 156
Gog, 83, 190
Golden altar, 69
Golden clouds, 7, 8, 22, 98, 121, 122, 136, 151, 158, 169, 182
Golden crown, 163, 183
Great Rift Valley, 111
Great Trumpet, 143

Halo, 98, 125, 136, 168
Hammer of the whole earth, 53, 140
Heaven, 95, 140, 170
Holy of Holies, 87
Holy Place, 59

Icarus, 79
Ice, 98, 125, 168
Idols, 75
Israel, 79, 82, 83, 130, 150, 166, 167, 191

Jasper, 114
Jericho, 86, 150
Jerusalem, 79, 81, 93, 142
Jesus Christ, the true God, 157
Josephus, 111
Joshua, 126

Judah, 103, 115
Judge angels, Israel, world, 190
Judgment, 72, 76, 188
Judgment of the Nations, 164
Judgment Seat of Christ, 164, 184, 190
Jupiter, 110

Key of the bottomless pit, 146
King of glory, 8
King of kings, 168, 177, 193
King of terrors, 151
King of the rock, 100
Kiyuwn, 152
Korah, 149

Lake of Fire, 165
Lamps, 24, 83, 114, 115
Lampstand, 127, 152, 153
Latter days, 64, 70
Laver, 145, 147
Levitical city, 137
Lord from heaven, 9
Lord's throne, 135
Lucifer, 111, 125, 146

Marriage in Cana, 91
Marriage of the Lamb, 90, 105, 164
Marriage Supper of the Lamb, 105, 164
Mediterranean Sea, 84
Melchisedec, 138
Mercy seat, 58, 65, 87

Meteorites, 43

Midnight, 175

Millennium, 70, 82, 103, 105, 155

Millstone, 72

Missile system, 108

Mitre, 112, 128

Morning star, 124, 125, 159, 175, 176

Mount of assembly, 146

Mystery, 17, 20

Naked-eye, 15, 22, 170, 175

Near Earth Asteroids, 87, 107, 129, 145

New Jerusalem, 11, 94, 141, 158, 177, 187

Nile River, 73, 82

Nineteen, 60

Noah, 169

Noise of his tabernacle, 89

Noonday, 94, 104

Omnipotence, 115

Opened my understanding, 31

Orbit, 43, 51, 79, 80, 87, 91, 103, 108, 118, 122, 126, 182, 188

Ornament, 137

Paradise, 11, 159

Passover, 105

Pattern, 18, 23, 36, 37, 49, 140

Pay-back, 90, 149

Peace, 61

Pearl of great price, 135, 158

Pentecost, 105, 175, 176

Petroleum industry, 113

Planet, 16, 152, 173

Planets, 43, 47, 48, 55, 56, 57, 58, 66, 80, 82, 90, 97, 137, 140, 151, 169, 170

Pope, 61

Putteth forth leaves, 60

Quarters, 14

Rahab, 43, 44, 45, 46, 47, 48, 72, 78, 79, 86, 100, 103, 117, 119, 125, 127, 135, 147, 154

Rainbow, 98, 103, 137, 168

Rapture, 4, 64, 105, 132, 146, 158, 159, 183, 184, 194

Rapture I, 93, 94

Rapture II, 93, 94, 183, 190

Reincarnation, 185

Restoration, 165

Ring, 99, 103, 115, 170, 172

San Juan Capistrano, 108

Sapphira, 134

Sapphire, 96, 98, 100, 103, 134, 136, 159

Satan, 47, 78, 79, 80, 86, 99, 101, 107, 125, 129, 146, 147, 165

Saturday Sabbath, 178

Saturn, 100, 115, 119, 121, 122, 127, 130, 133, 135, 136, 137, 140, 142, 152, 159, 169, 170, 171, 172, 175, 176, 182

Saturn's day, 178

Saved by fire, 76
Sea of glass, 98, 115
Second Advent, 85, 165
Secret of his tabernacle, 92
Secrets of wisdom, 60
Seraphim, 23, 27, 117, 119, 120, 193
Seven, 101, 159
Seven eyes, 126
  months, 85, 164, 189
  trumpet judgments, 83
Seventieth Week of Daniel, 62, 167
Sheep, 164
Sickle, 183, 187
Sign of the End of the Age, 166, 186
  of the Son of Man, 105
Sion, 158
Sirius, 173
Six-Day War, 61, 70
Sodom and Gomorrah, 110
Solar system, 141, 152, 170, 173
Sphere, 13, 22, 57, 117
STAR OF YOUR GOD, 152
Station, 80
Stone tablet, 187
Stones of fire, 80
Strange act, 54
Strong meat, 160
Sword, 33, 37, 66, 83, 110, 147, 155

Tabernacle, 29, 36, 38, 39, 40, 47, 48, 49, 58, 67, 84, 93, 106, 122, 127, 128, 139, 145, 151, 152, 153

Table of Shewbread, 147
Temple, 84, 93, 128
Third heaven, 11, 22, 123, 136, 141, 147, 152
Three are one, 179
Time of Jacob's trouble, 92, 93, 162
  of the end, 60
Times of the Gentiles, 60, 63
Tisha Be'Av, 110
Transfiguration, 178
Transparent glass, 158
Trap, 151
Tribulation, 37, 62, 71, 76, 79, 82, 92, 93, 167, 183, 186
Tsunami, 83

Unleavened Bread, 105
Upside down, 45, 150

Vatican, 61
Vengeance, 69, 70, 71, 84, 92, 164
Vengeance is mine, 149

Wheel, 26, 50, 51, 55, 103, 116, 182, 188
Whirlwind, 130
Wings of a dove, 173
Wormwood, 80, 99, 125, 131, 146
Wrath, 73

Y'shua, 134
Yahweh, 134
Year, 165
  of recompenses, 113